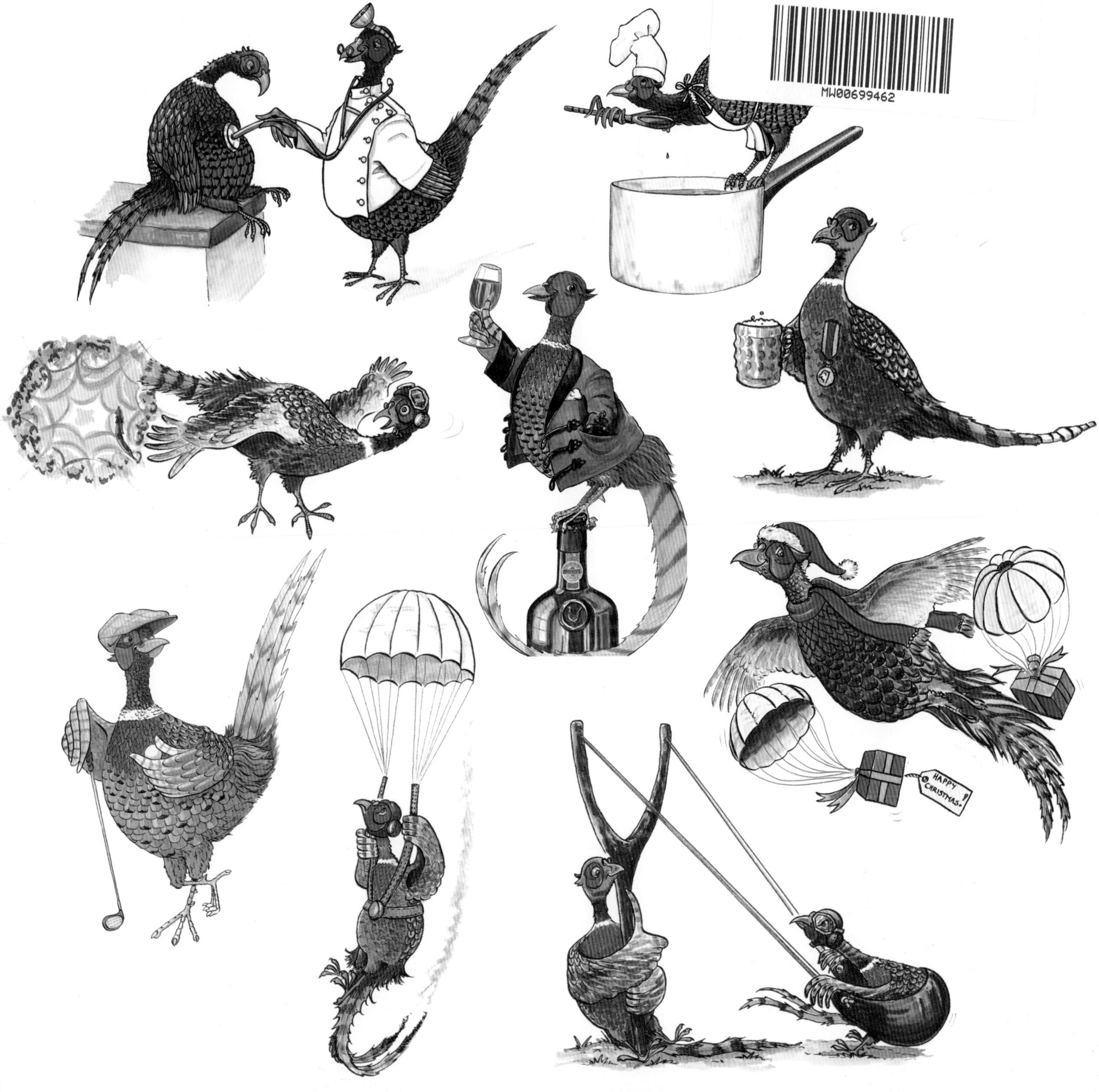
HAPPY CHRISTMAS!

MAD DOGS AND ENGLISHMEN

MAD DOGS AND ENGLISHMEN

SHOOTING CARTOONS BY BRYN PARRY

SWAN·HILL
PRESS

With love to Emma, Sophie, Tom, Louisa,
Mango and Pickle –
and the rest of the family

Text and illustrations Copyright © 2001 Bryn Parry
'Shooting Types' text Copyright © Giles Catchpole

First published in the UK in 2001 by Swan Hill Press, an
imprint of Quiller Publishing Ltd.

Fourth impression 2002

British Library Cataloguing-in-Publication Data
   A catalogue record for this book
   is available from the British Library

ISBN 1 84037 232 X

Typeset by Rowland Phototypesetting Ltd, Bury St Edmunds,
Suffolk.
Printed in China

Swan Hill Press
an imprint of Quiller Publishing Ltd.
Wykey House, Wykey, Shrewsbury, SY4 1JA, England

CONTENTS

Introduction

This is a book of very few words. Not only because I can't spell or write proper but also because I wanted it to be a book of cartoons. Nevertheless, I'll cram a few words in here so that you can make a choice; to glance at them or get on to the drawings – either way I hope that you enjoy my doodles.

I have been doodling away all my life and am rather pleased and not a little amazed to be able to make a living from my hobby. I have always felt that to draw was not as good as an ability to run fast, to hit a cricket ball or indeed to shoot straight, but now I am not so sure. When I see the sort of jobs that most of my sporty friends have settled into, I begin to feel that those days hiding in the art department to avoid the cross-country run were days well spent.

This book is about men and dogs and shooting. I first borrowed a shotgun in 1990, having been happy with a rifle since I was eight. The whole concept of swinging through and lead were a total mystery and the woods were filled with the cackling laughter of pheasants and the dark curses of Bryn. I now understand the principles but can assure any pheasants reading this that I am still way behind successfully putting them into practice. The frustration that I feel when I miss yet again or the expression on Mango (the Labrador's) face when we are standing at the edge of a wood and it is precipitating down are my inspirations. I doubt that I'll ever be a good shot any more than Mango will be the perfect gun dog but I, we, love it.

I get so excited the night before a good day's shooting that I cannot sleep for the thumping of my heart and the whooshing of blood around my adrenalised brain. I love seeing the characters as they arrive in their cars and clobber, the mad dogs, wild children and worried organisers. I love the joshing between guns as yet another bird flies down the line flicking into a victory roll and the smug faces of the beaters who know they would have done better. I love the way we are all levelled by the mud and mire; the captain of industry no better than the bedraggled spaniel and the Keeper more important than a King. I love the excitement of the birds coming over and the oh, too rare, moment as one folds and then the satisfaction of the dog retrieving it. Finally I love the jokes at lunch, the feeling of invincibility if I've been shooting well (I won't mention the utter gloom if I haven't) and the happy, tired face of a dog who for once has earned her supper. I love it all.

I'll let you get on with the book as I assume that you love it as well or you would not be reading this, but before I do, may I make one little plea? My son Tom also loves his shooting and wiped my eye with his .410 when he was nine. I hope that if he has a boy he will have the chance to let him take up shooting should he wish, and to share in the sport we have so enjoyed. I hope that you will continue to support our rights to shoot and to carry that message to anyone who should seek to prevent it.

Lastly, talking of support, I'd like to thank my wife Emma who thought she was marrying a career soldier and had a sporting chance of being Lady Emma, the General's wife . . . oops, . . . sorry and thanks!

Bryn Parry

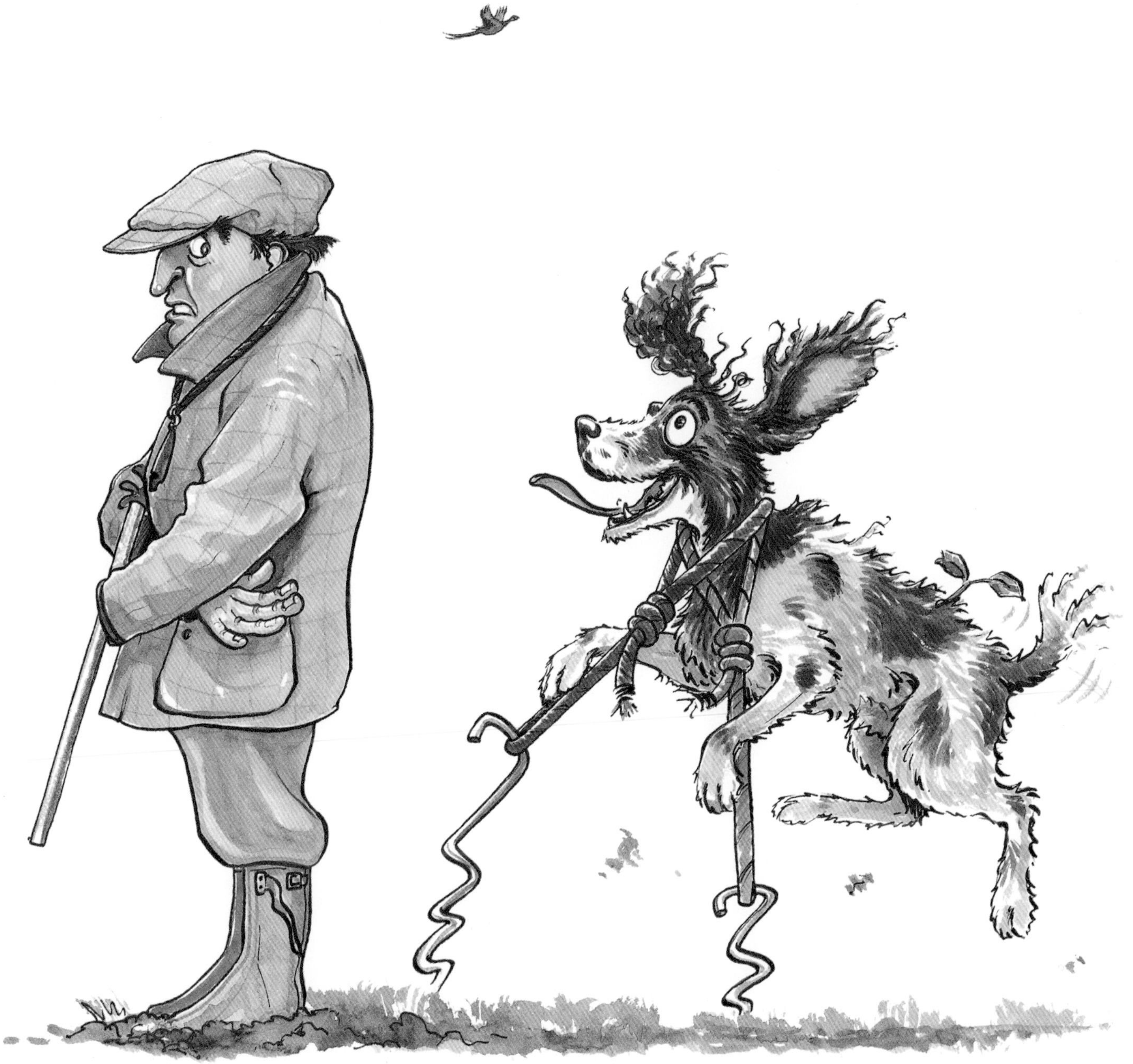

MAD DOG AND ENGLISHMAN

CHAPTER 1

Rules of the Game

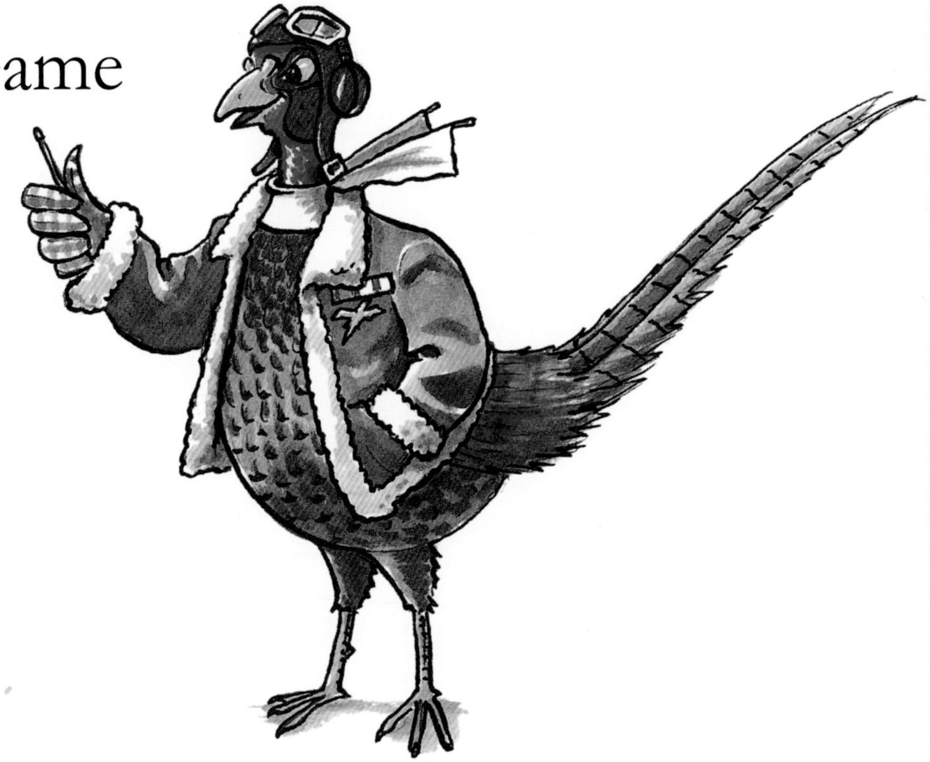

RULE ONE

Guns must remain in their slips between drives

RULE TWO

Guns must be broken at the end of the drive

RULE THREE

Strictly no running in

RULE FOUR

Take care when guns are loaded

RULE FIVE

No picking up before the whistle

RULE SIX

Non-toxic shot is obligatory on duck . . . cartridges can be supplied

RULE SEVEN

The end of the drive will be signalled by a whistle

RULE EIGHT

Partridges: please ignore the English and concentrate on the Frenchmen

RULE NINE

Ear defenders are absolutely essential

RULE TEN

Never mix bores

RULE ELEVEN

No ground game

RULE TWELVE

Please remember your peg number

A FATHER'S ADVICE

If a sportsman true you'd be
Listen carefully to me

Never, never let your gun
Pointed be at anyone
That it might unloaded be
Matters not the least to me

When a ditch or fence you cross
Though of time it cause you loss
From your gun the cartridge take
For the greater safety sake

If 'twixt you and neighbouring gun
Bird may fly or beast may run
Let this maxim e're be thine ~
Follow not across the line

Stops and beaters oft unseen
Lurk behind some leafy screen
Calm and steady always be
Never shoot where you can't see

Keep your place and silent be
Game can hear and game can see
Don't be greedy, better spared
Is a pheasant than one shared

You may kill or you may miss
But at all times think of this
All the pheasants ever bred
Won't repay for one man dead

Choosing the Perfect Dog

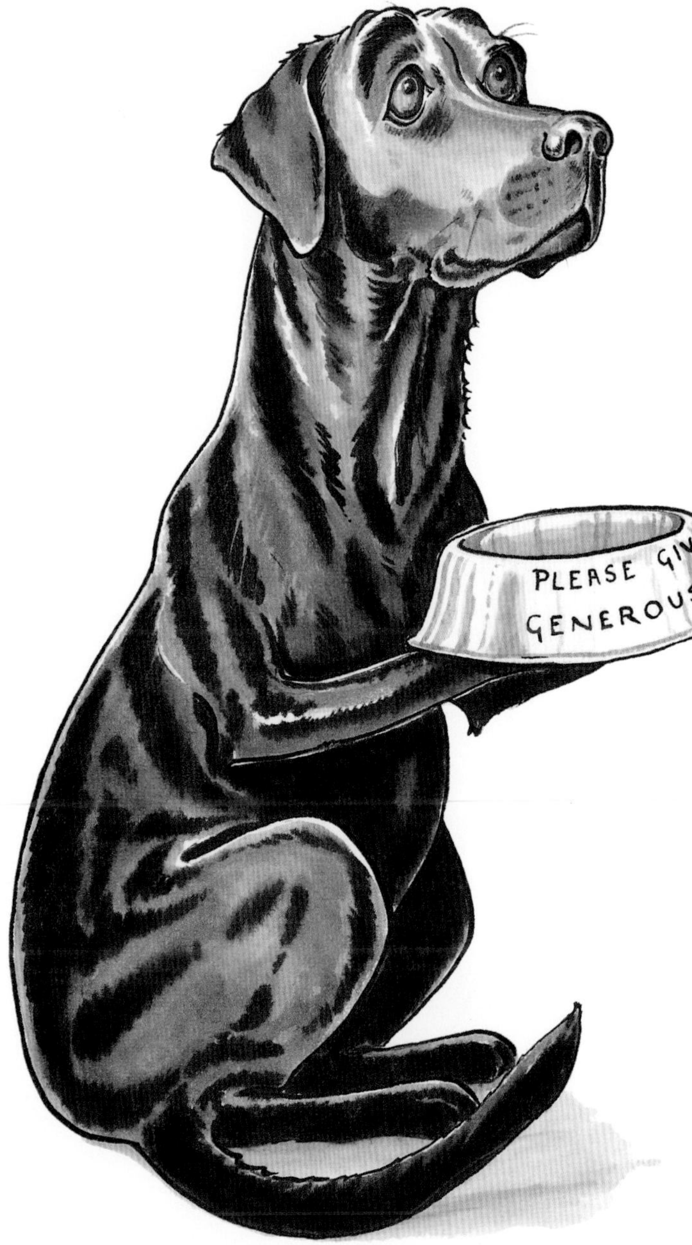
PLEASE GIVE
GENEROUSLY

Lunchtime Labrador

MELLOW YELLOW

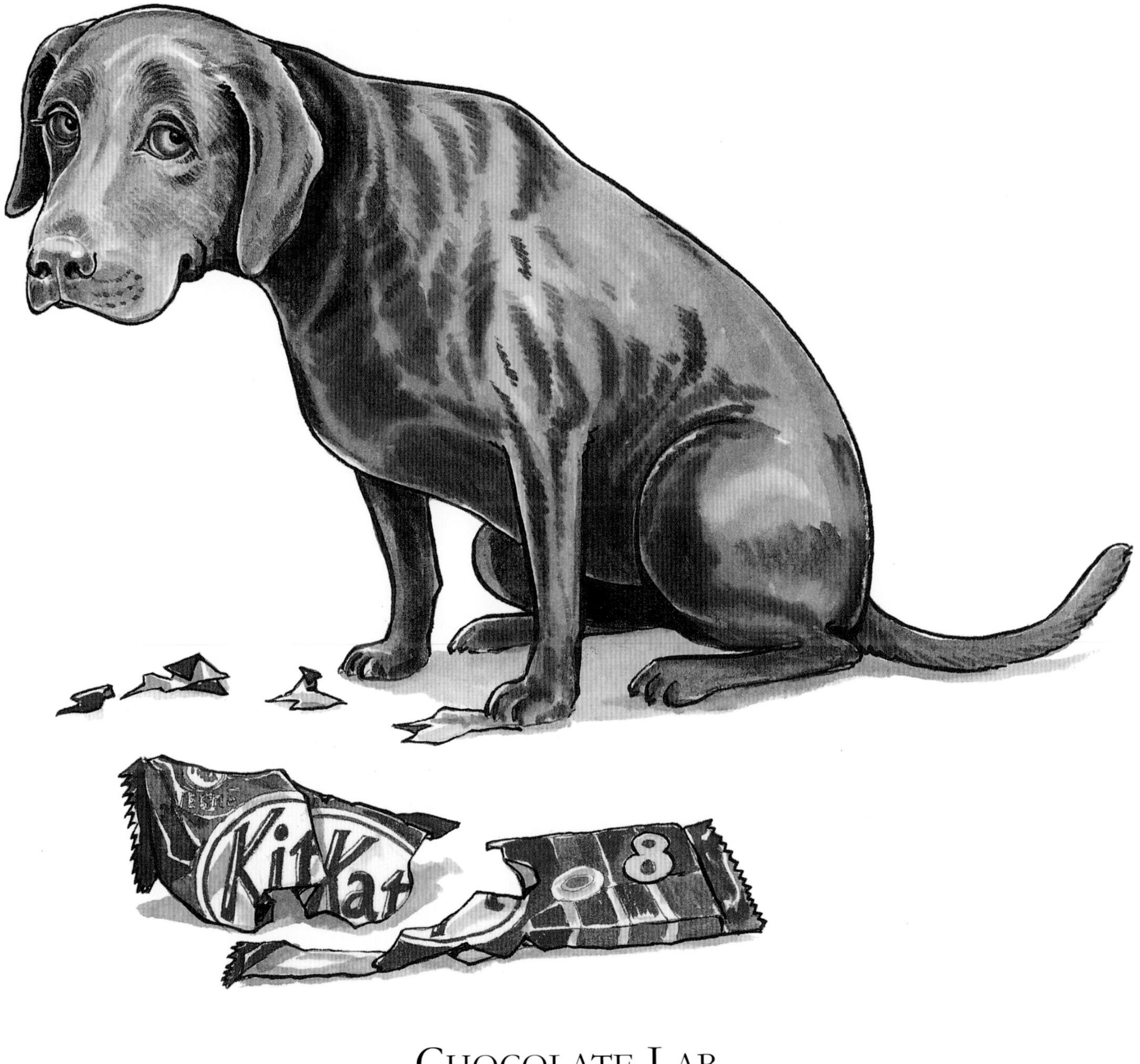
KitKat
8

Chocolate Lab

WOCKER COCKER

SPRINGER

SUPERIOR SETTER

PERPLEXED POINTER

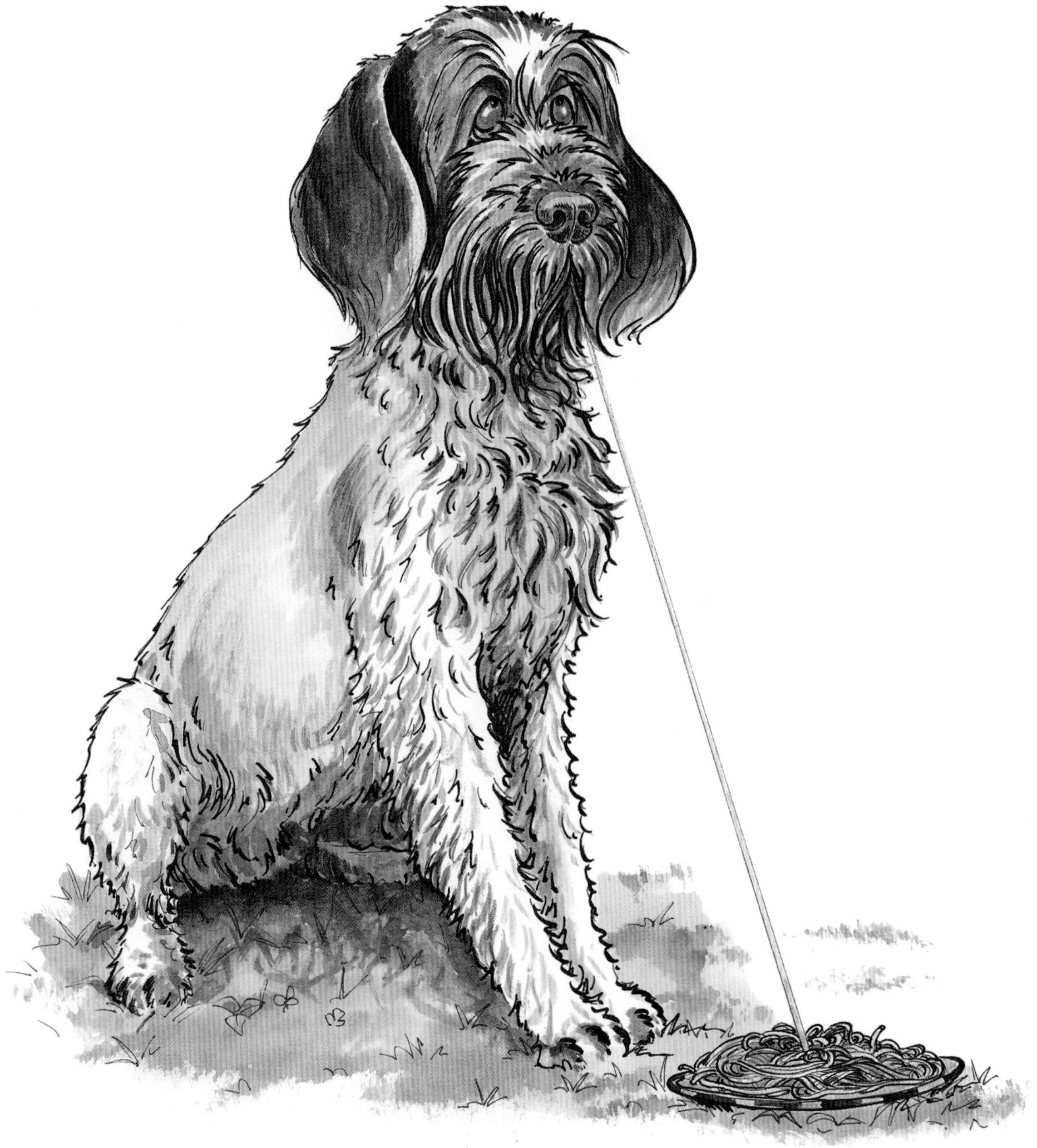

Spaghetti Spinone

. . . and other Sporting Dogs . . .

TETHERED TERRIER

PARSON JACK RUSSELL

NORFOLK TERRIER

WEST HIGHLAND TERRIER

BORDER TERRIER

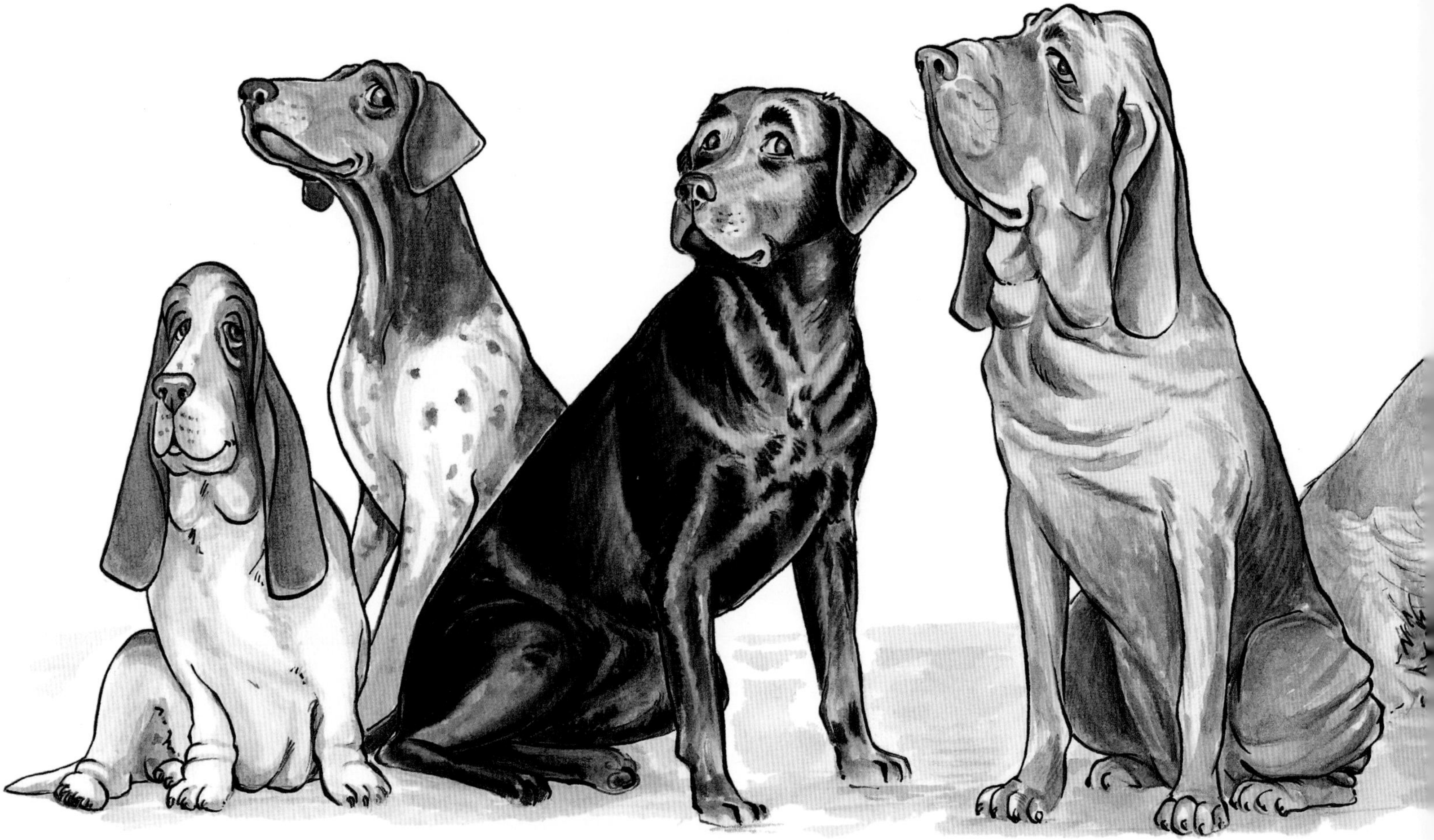

Pedigrees .....

. . . . . AND CHUM!

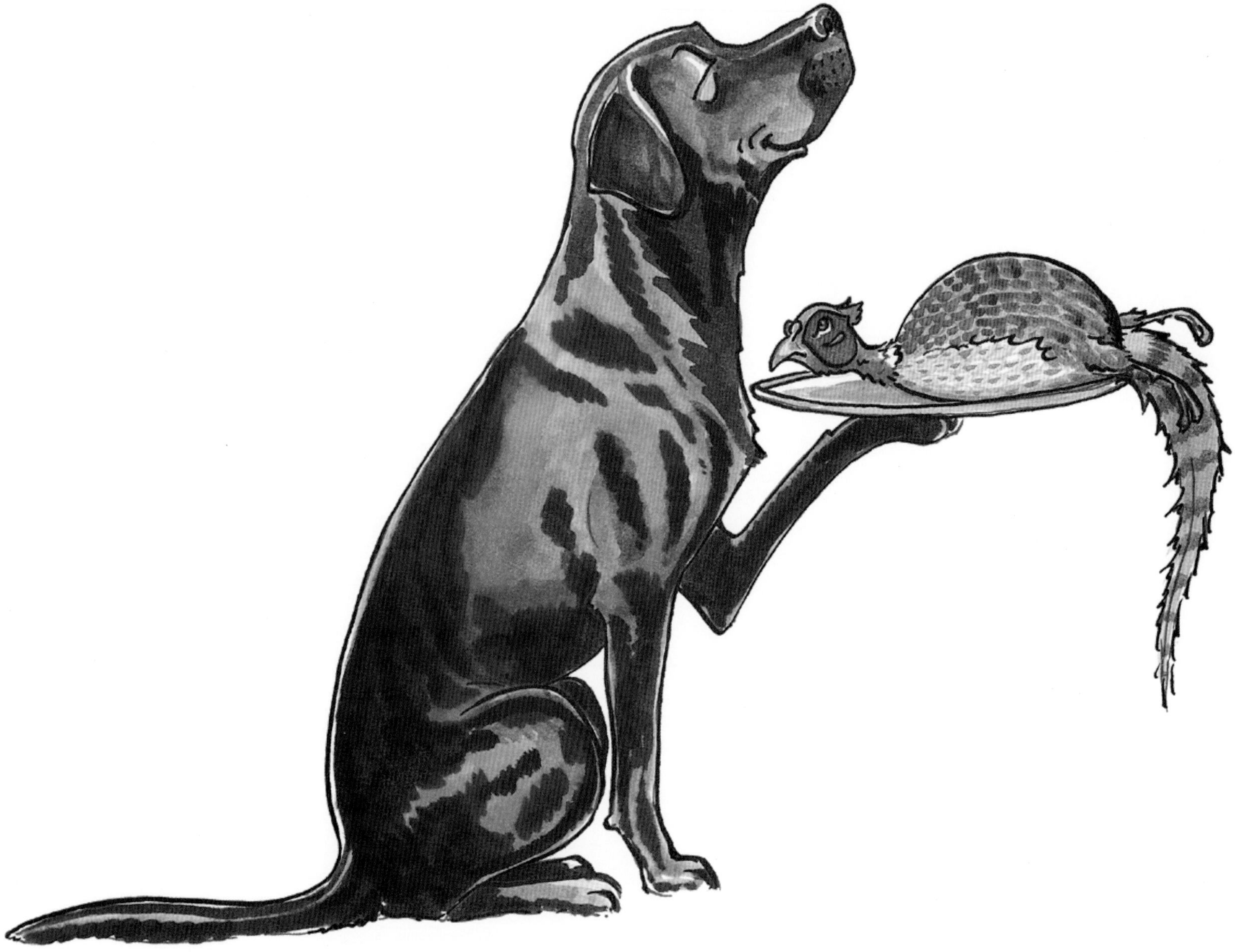

Good Dog . . . . .

. . . . . BAD DOG!

THE PERFECT GUN DOG

Chapter 3

Shooting Types

The New Gun
And some Shooting Types . . . . .

THE OLDER GUN

He mistook the Ark for a game-cart and lobbed in his brace of birds with a brisk word of congratulation to Noah about the straightness of his beating line. He has fought in more wars than you could shake a stick at, and has won most of the important ones more or less single-handed. He tends towards the view that young people would be well advised to spend a little time between school and university finding themselves a decent war to get mixed up in, since it gives a sense of perspective later in life. A combination of the dicky hip, sundry wounds, chronic but intermittent gout and a lifelong addiction to rough-cut shag means that he is incapable of moving to any outlying peg and the role of walking Gun is a mystery to him. He puts 5,000 rounds a season through his old Holland, which his grandfather, secure in the knowledge that the thing was within a micron of being out of proof then and was a liability to anyone within thirty yards, presented him as a gift on his 21st birthday, and which has not been within a mile of a smith's since.

No one can remember when he joined the team, or whether he ever did. When they turned up to shoot, there he was, and he has been coming ever since. There may very well be another shoot on the estate next door who are still waiting for him and wondering if it was something they said.

He shoots from a stick and he seldom misses. Not that he lets off terribly often. Many years of patience spent behind a rock or in a trench or up a tree waiting for some variety of foreigner to stick his head into view has given him a very clear picture of the right moment to participate.

Accordingly he demolishes a limited number of selected birds – presumably those with a goodly quantity of white to their eye – and ignores the rest, be they high, wide or handsome. Since he is – selectively – as deaf as a post to boot, yelling at him that there are birds roaring past, over or by him will do no good at all. He has been shooting here since before you were born and knows every drive like the back of his hand. Backwards, forwards and sideways. When the keeper attempts a brave new departure by reversing one of the main drives, he will snort derisively, announce loudly that every pheasant in the place will leg it up the side hedge if you try it that way, and spend the whole of the next drive fiddling with his pipe. The fact that he has been shooting here since before you were born and has seen all the drives under every circumstance and that he is almost certainly right only serves to make this habit more annoying.

Equally he has a habit of cornering the younger Guns after shooting and embarking upon his life story. Unfortunately he always chooses the one day when you absolutely, positively must get away upon pain of death and so you cut him short to your embarrassment and his chagrin. Which is a pity, because you don't get the chance every day of the week to meet the man who slept with Mata Hari, rode with Lawrence, blew up Rommel's fuel dumps, did time garrotting bad hats in the Balkans, hunted with Hemingway, double-dated with Erroll Flynn, invented the telescopic sight and designed a salmon fly so lethal that it was banned by Act of Parliament.

Shooting Types text by Giles Catchpole

THE BELTED EARL

Also known to his intimates as 'the Belting Earl' on account of his habit of belting birds at prodigious distances which have dodged his neighbour's neighbour's gun. He never practises because, what with his own moor behind one castle and the sumptuous pheasant shoot in front of the other, he scarcely has the time. And that is before the invitations. With five days on the driving moor and the schedule in the park he issues a fair old stack of shooting invites himself every season and notwithstanding the numbers of relatives and business guests upon whom he bestows them, several dozen guests are likely to invite him back. Most of these are other belted earls, so that the season is a long round of moated manors, battlemented castles and sundry assorted gamebirds scudding, flaring and soaring as season and species require.

He manages to shoot both diffidently and well. In between slotting the highest and fastest and apologetically 'tidying up' behind – a long way behind – most of the rest of the line, he spends much of the time on his peg arguing with the scruffy dogs who accompany him everywhere and which tend to be the result of an unguarded moment between the castle kennels and a passing stranger of indeterminate parentage who accompanied the man who came to mend the roof of the west wing. The Countess, whose hobby is the careful and selected breeding and training of peerless retrievers was naturally mortified, but the Belted Earl took a fancy to the offspring, and promptly adopted one as his personal mascot. In a couple of generations the Labshund or the Terraniel will be a must-have fashion accessory among *Hello!* readers. The family motto ('Suffer the Lowly') may be variously interpreted as welcoming scruffy dogs onto the sofa of the Chinese Green Velvet Drawing Room, or having to put up with the coach-loads of tourists who spend the summer traipsing round whichever castle the Belted Earl is not presently inhabiting. So the estates wash their collective faces and the tourists keep the castles roofed and wired, which leaves the Belted Earl free to sit on the board of sundry companies which make useful investments in software companies in California, where a title opens more doors than you could shake a coronet at, which periodically float at shocking subscription levels, leaving the Belted Earl as surprised as anyone but considerably richer than most. And which allows him to shoot most days during the season, which is why he shoots so well, and how he became known as the Belting Earl, which is where we came in.

LIKE A MILITARY OPERATION

He says nine-fifteen for nine-thirty, but he means 09:00 hours for 09:07, given that a kettle takes four minutes to boil, if watched, and the resulting coffee will take six minutes to cool to an average 68° in order to be drinkable by an average human being; which leaves three minutes to make the brew-up and ten to swallow it assuming average pace being maintained all round. OK? This means that the first drive can be blanking in at 08:45, on the basis that the birds will congregate in the pines at 09:25 and can be held there by the stops for ten minutes only which requires us to be on our pegs and ready at 09:35 for a first flush at approximately 09:36.30. Right. Any questions?

Perhaps he was an artillery commander before he accumulated the estate, and perhaps whole regiments depended for their lives on the split-second timing of his salvoes, fusillades and barrages; but do I really need this now? Quite often, it has nothing whatever to do with military training and much to do with some management consultancy course that pointed out that you should always hire the candidate with the tidiest desk. This guy sharpens his pencils every evening in order to leave the mornings free for really important tasks like polishing his stapler.

Now it is perhaps unnecessarily cruel to pick on the generalissimo in this way. He has after all invited us, or at least let us on the place under whatever terms and conditions; but

he has forgotten the central issue rather, which is that the day should, after all is said and done, be fun. And that is kind of difficult if you are being harried from pillar to post hither and yon and being given wholly unintelligible instructions as to what to do when you get there.

'Follow the hedge-line up to the apex and stand 43 yards due south of the *Arboris giganticus* at map reference 100985. After three minutes or 10:31 hours, whichever is the later, move 80 yards east by magnetic north or away from the nearest beater. Don't, whatever you do, shoot before then or you will ruin everything. Understood?' In a pig's eye.

The principal difficulty he consistently overlooks is that we are dealing here with birds and animals and beaters and, to be frank – us. And few of the above will conform to the strict regimentation he is inclined to inflict. Especially after lunch. Chaos theory dictates that the greater and more rigid the control that is placed upon fluid or organic entities, the greater their likely divergence from the plan once left to their own devices. More or less. Which means that the Guns are usually facing in the wrong direction behind the wrong hedge, the birds have all legged it down the ditch towards the spinney and the beaters are having a smoke in the wrong wood while waiting for the keeper to blow the whistle he has left at home down the walkie-talkie that the host has left on the dashboard of the game cart in the first place.

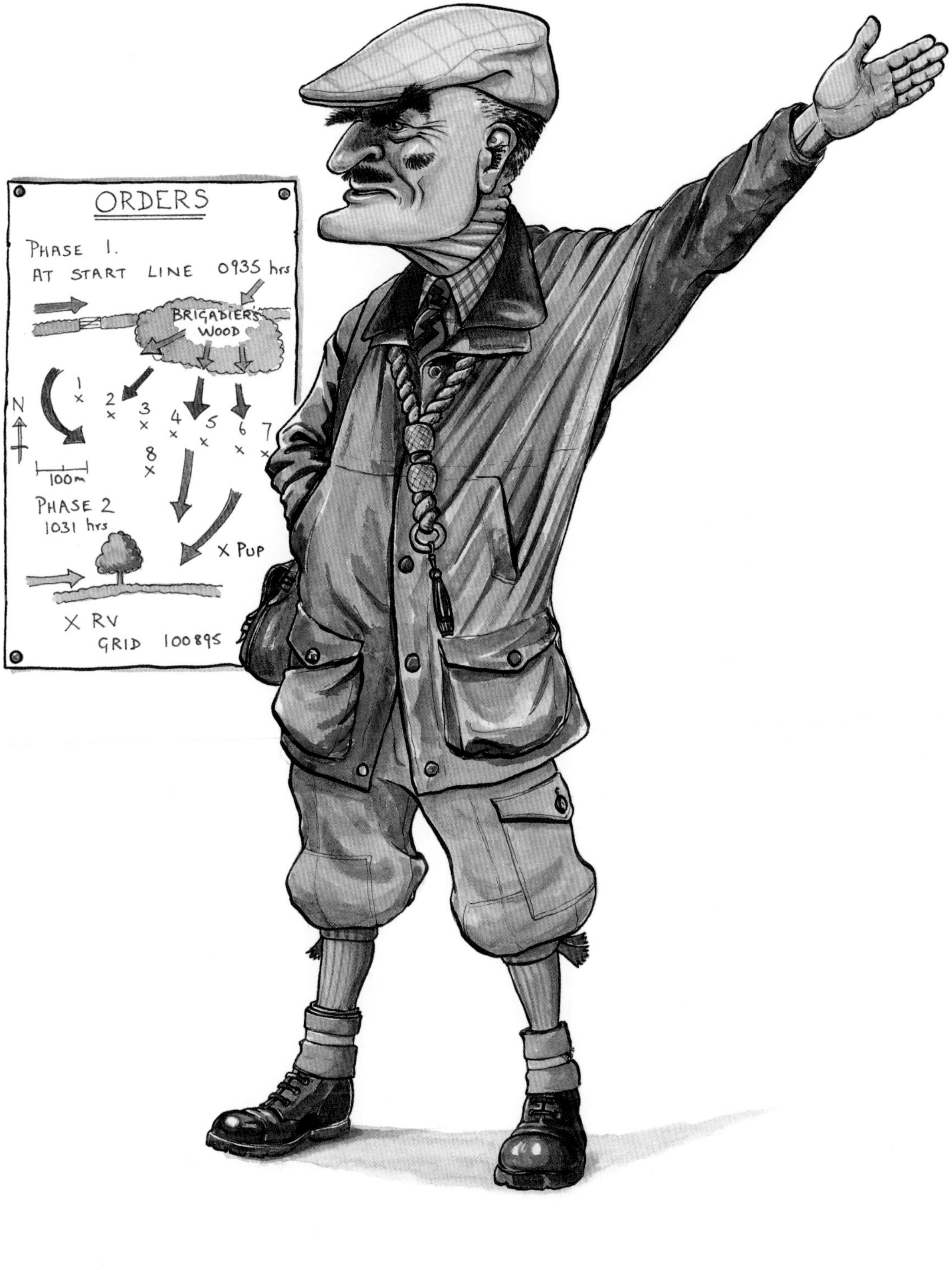
ORDERS
PHASE 1.
AT START LINE 0935 hrs
BRIGADIER'S WOOD
N
1 2 3 4 5 6 7 8
100m
PHASE 2
1031 hrs
X PUP
X RV
GRID 100895

THE OLD-STYLE KEEPER

He bunked off school aged nine and three-quarters to collect eggs for the head keeper's bantams when the Euston System was an innovation. After being routinely thrashed by teacher and parents he variously decked the one and left the other to become deputy assistant apprentice to the junior deputy under-keeper on an outlying beat of the estate just before the war. Exactly which war is an issue into which it is best not to probe too deeply, but the odds are that it involved red tunics and the rapid formation of squares. After which, the bulk of the keepering staff having been wiped out, he was promoted to beat-keeper by the present owner's grandfather – 'the Major' – and received the princely wages of six shillings a week, a cottage, a new suit and a bucket of beer on quarter-days. Following his single-handed destruction of a gang of poachers with a tent-peg, a ball of string and his fists, his talents were recognised and on the retirement of the legendary head keeper Jack 'Rabbit' Skinner shortly after the next war, he was made head keeper by the then young 'Colonel'.

Much has changed, of course, but certain principles yet hold. Despite being as old as the hills, he will still confront any 'Gyppos' and 'Diddicoys' who venture onto the estate and establish their obedience to his supremacy by giving the headman a good kicking. He goes on poacher patrol nightly and while he leans more heavily on his stick than once he did, it is as feared in the vicinity as the tent-peg ever was. He still consumes his bucket of beer at regular intervals and if you can catch him in the mood after it, he will share with you the secrets of running a successful shoot, how to rear partridges against the odds and how to make a pheasant fly though the eye of a needle. Add another pint and he'll tell you why he has been happily married for six decades or more, how to charm a fox to within stroking distance and the real reason why a visiting Gun sent him a pair of Boss sidelocks as a gesture of appreciation.

On shoot days he is immediately identifiable by the shininess of his boots, the cut of his suit and his trademark stiff collar. His manoeuvres, all of which are recorded in a notebook and rehearsed at length with the Boss, key stops and flankers the evening before a shoot day, take into account wind direction, sun, topography, date, air temperature, ground temperature, and above all his opinion of the Guns. Each drive is well practised and executed with a minimum of noise except for the steady tap-tap-tap of the beaters' sticks. His days are always successful. Some are great, but none fail. He does not expect to be tipped, but accepts such offerings as the Guns offer. On one notable occasion, however, after a pheasant day that could only be described as spectacular, he was moved to comment. Without so much as a glance at the tip he had received as he handed a visiting Gun his brace, and which he could feel was as inadequate for the quality of the day as the Gun's shooting had been, he held out his closed fist and pressed the contents back into the miscreant's hand, announcing loudly 'If that's your idea of gratitude, young man, I'll settle for respect.' Which is as it should be.

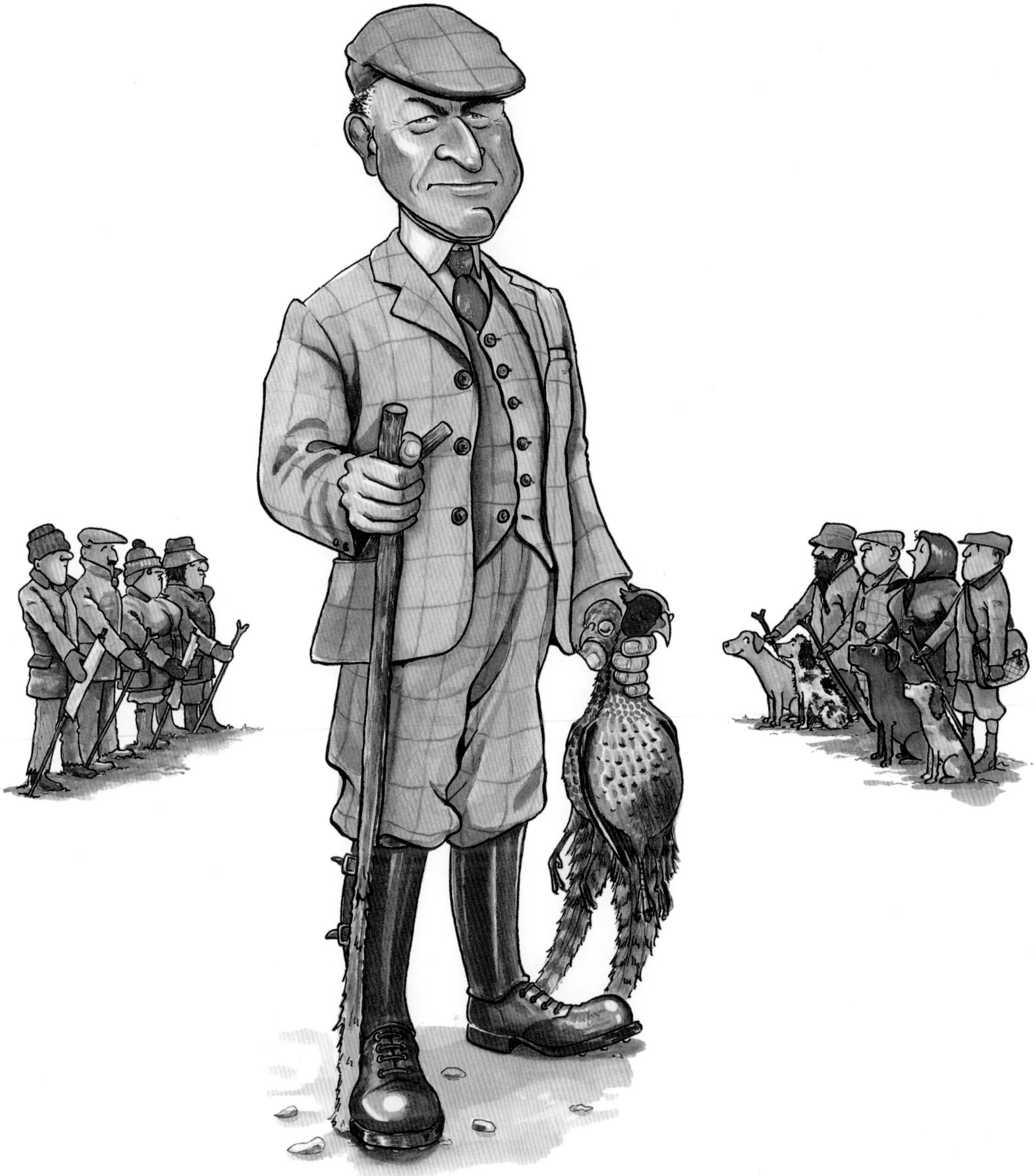

THE LADY SHOT

When her late husband, bless him, not the latest late one, but an earlier late one, asked what she wanted as a wedding present she never hesitated for a moment. 'Boss . . . ' she said and that was all he needed to hear. She might have meant boscage in reference to the front garden or indeed Boston, Mass. for the honeymoon on Cape Cod; but the upshot was a nice pair of sixteens which she uses today with no less effectiveness and delight than the day they arrived – oh, more years ago than she cares to remember, or you to ask, if you know what's good for you.

She has many skills, and if you look at the wedding photographs, the early ones . . . well, any of them actually, you will recognise that she had, has had, has still much else besides. Her only failing seems to have been losing husbands. Admittedly if they lead from the front storming things in whatever war is current, hunt three days a week, and big game at that, and drive fast cars at weekends while living on a diet of red meat, whisky and cigars there is a tendency towards early departure. Still, live fast, die young, shed a tear and move on. All girls want today is a flat, a job and a pension. Don't know they're born.

Still, along the way the husbands provided sufficiently in many respects. The moor though she brought with her as a dowry – each time – and it remains her pride and joy. She knows it probably better than she knew any husband, but then she has had it longer. And God help any keeper or guest who can't keep up with her as she pounds about after the grouse in summer or the stags in the autumn – or for that matter the hinds in deepest winter. She and her stalker are legends on the hill both together and separately and stories abound concerning their forays after the hinds in the corries in the snow.

She is formidable on the low ground too. Quite apart from her manifest skill and the fact that her invitation both back and forth has been an annual event for the best part of two generations already, she is good company and a wise counsel. Her stories can bring a tint to the cheek of the most hardened beater. Many a young keeper has benefited from her brief comments following this drive or that, and many an old keeper, for that matter, has bathed in her compliments and the congratulations of others, having put her advice into practice. She has a knack for spotting where birds will go that comes with years of experience, and will often mooch a few yards off her peg at the end of a line of Guns to act as unofficial stop by the corner. Not that so doing will stop her reaching out and demolishing that soaring archangel that her neighbour has just given up on as being too, too high.

She's no slouch indoors either, actually, and while she can convulse the company with charades after her dram, it would be a brave man who played her ton-up in the billiards room for a quid a point, regardless of the time of day. They say it would take a brave man to let her name the stakes, as a matter of fact, or the game, when the candles and the decanter are low enough at the end of shooting day. They say. Men today! Boys! Don't know they're born.

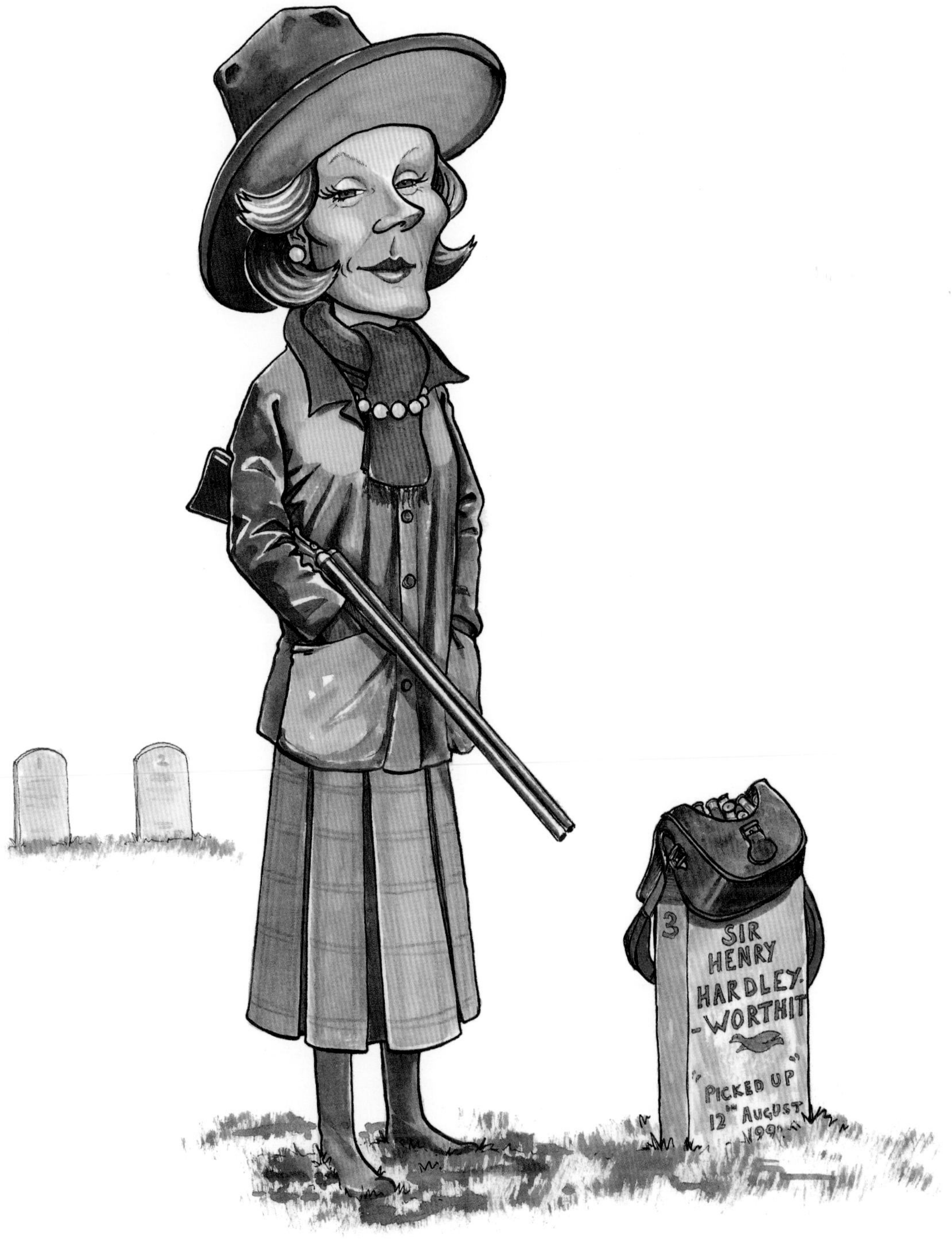
3
SIR HENRY HARDLEY-WORTHIT
"PICKED UP"
12th AUGUST

THE COURT JESTER

There's usually one in every beating line. If you are lucky he will be a complete stranger, who will none the less be ready with a comment on the performance of the Guns in general. If you are unfortunate, he will know you as an individual and will take the mickey out of your personal performance throughout the day with more remorseless accuracy than you will be able to muster under the circumstances. 'Well, well, boys, now we shall see something. The finest team of game shooters in the country. Sorry, that's next week isn't it? So who have we here then? Har, Har, Har.' And once it has started, you can be sure it will carry on all day. 'What was wrong with that cock bird, lads? Perhaps it was a stealth bomber then? Har, Har, Har.' This is the clown who shouts 'Over!' when the tail-less hen pheasant comes to you during the partridge drive, and gets you every time. This is the joker who calls 'Back! Back!' when you are just in the middle of a quiet pee behind a tree after lunch. This is the commentator who asserts after the elevenses break that 'I hope he's had a good pull at yon flask. He shoots a good deal better when he's had a decent gargle', thereby suggesting that you are a duffer for the most part and a chronic alcoholic for the rest.

Even if you are shooting well, it is no defence. When you have just nailed a serious archangel, he will ask loudly if you failed to see the high bird that went by above it. As you are congratulating yourself on a stonking right-and-left, he will announce that he has seen a shot aimed at one bird hit another before, but he has seldom seen it occur twice so

close together. And if you are drawn as a walking Gun, you need be in no doubt as to who will be strolling up the edge of the wood next to you. 'Not too fast through here then, lads. If we tire him out too early on, he may never shoot anything at all. Har, Har, Har. Coming left! Oops! Were we not ready there, Sir? Har, Har, Har.' As a matter of fact, this is your chance for a modest revenge. If the gods are on your side, and the birds are feeling co-operative, there will be a steady stream of opportunities for you. Clear the mind. Focus on the birds. And carry plenty of cartridges. Pass the first one to him as you pick it up. Deliver the second brace with a wry smile. Ask him to pick up the next two or three himself when he catches up with the rest of the line. Drop the first part of the next right-and-left just behind him when he's made it back, and the second a good way beyond that and ask him to fetch it. Preferably from a thorn bush. And then drop one on his head as he is poking about in the brambles. As the drive continues you can ask him loudly if he is managing by himself, or if he wants a boy to come and lend a hand. As he stumbles along the track in your wake, you may enquire if he wants you to wait or whether he will be arriving before the next drive. And when he does finally stagger up towards the game-cart, laden with your birds and breathing hard through the stick between his teeth, you can hand him the last bird with a flourish and say quietly 'Well, we seem to have scrambled one down there, don't we? Har, Har, Har.' Well, it's a nice thought anyway.

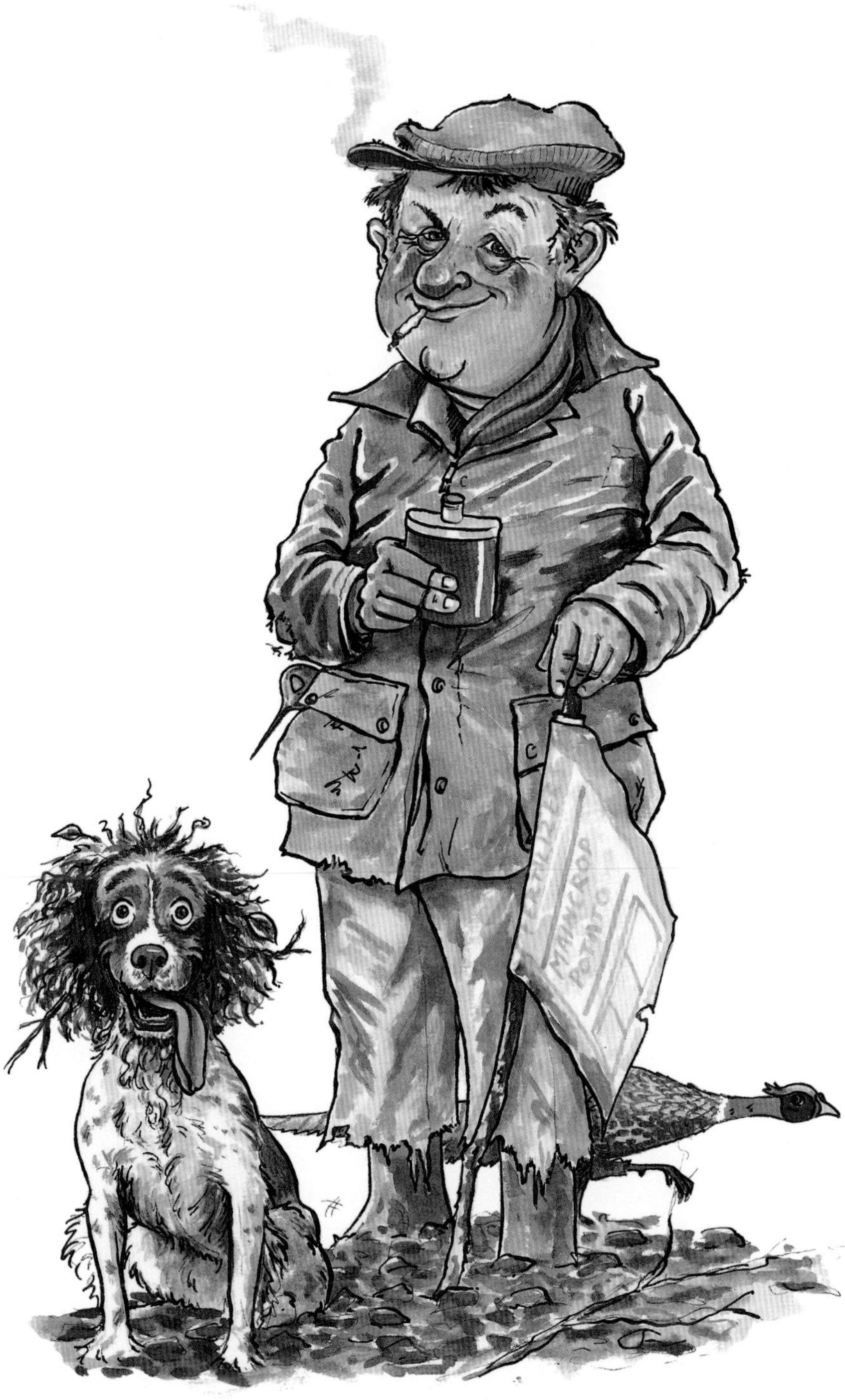
MAINCROP
POTATO

THE DANGEROUS SHOT

From the moment he exits the car, which he has parked so as to block in the game-cart, you know that he is a nightmare in knickerbockers. Even as he puts the gun together the muzzles are swinging round and about at navel level and as he attaches the sprightly springer to his cartridge belt with a long cord you realise that the full horror knows no bounds. How he has reached this point there is no knowing. Perhaps he was never taught properly in the first place. Maybe his age and status in other parts of life have protected him, for some reason, from the proper reproofs, dressing-downs and simple bawling-outs which might have exorcised the demons at an earlier and less entrenched stage. But now the monster is complete and the innocent within irrecoverable.

He has no slip, sleeve or cover for his gun which is carted from drive to drive either at the trail, pointing at the knees of those in front, or balanced on his shoulder, triggers down, so that those behind are confronted by the menace of his bores. He never opens it, in either event. What he does do, though, is to clamp it periodically in the crook of one elbow or other while he hauls at the sprightly springer which has wrapped itself round legs of others and himself. As he whirls about to undo the resultant tangle, those muzzles are circling too, addressing an eye here, a shoulder there and the napes of those who have turned away aghast.

And this is before we have even reached the pegs. Once there, he extracts the woolly oil mop from the chamber of his choke barrel, commenting that he has been looking for that for ages. It is replaced by cartridges. Once comprehensively loaded, he cradles the piece across his chest, changing side from time to time in order to give both his neighbours equal opportunity to stare down those black holes.

When the birds put in an appearance the thing is almost unwatchable. Ignoring anything at a respectable height, he addresses those birds which hop the hedge behind which the beaters are approaching. As he focuses gimlet eyes on his chosen target the springer gathers itself to earn its title. As the bird skims the furze the dog launches itself into the retrieve as the owner slips off the safety catch. The dog reaches the end of its string as the Gun reaches the climax of his swing. Both dog and man end up flat on their backs in the mud. The bird passes unscathed, but as shocked as anyone and the shot goes . . . who knows? Off. Away. Somewhere. A better place. With one knee and one hand still on the sod he tries to get off a second barrel at the departing quarry so that the pickers-up are not left out of the proceedings, but he is frustrated once more by the spaniel, which is now seeking to make amends for its behaviour by trying to lick the mud from his master's face. Roaring at the dog he hefts to his feet and straightens his belt. Ignoring the tuft of grass which now sprouts from his muzzles, he reloads and settles down once more. Then spotting the possible obstruction he sticks a finger down the sharp end and wiggles it about. Then he rests the butt on his boot, as the springer gambols, and squints down the tubes to make sure they are clear of turf. Reassured, he once more assumes the ready position. It is not yet ten o'clock. He rummages in his pocket for his flask. Faint. Feign a coronary. Food poisoning. Galloping dysentery. Divorce. Anything. Get out. Go home. Save yourself. All the pheasants ever bred. Especially if it's you.

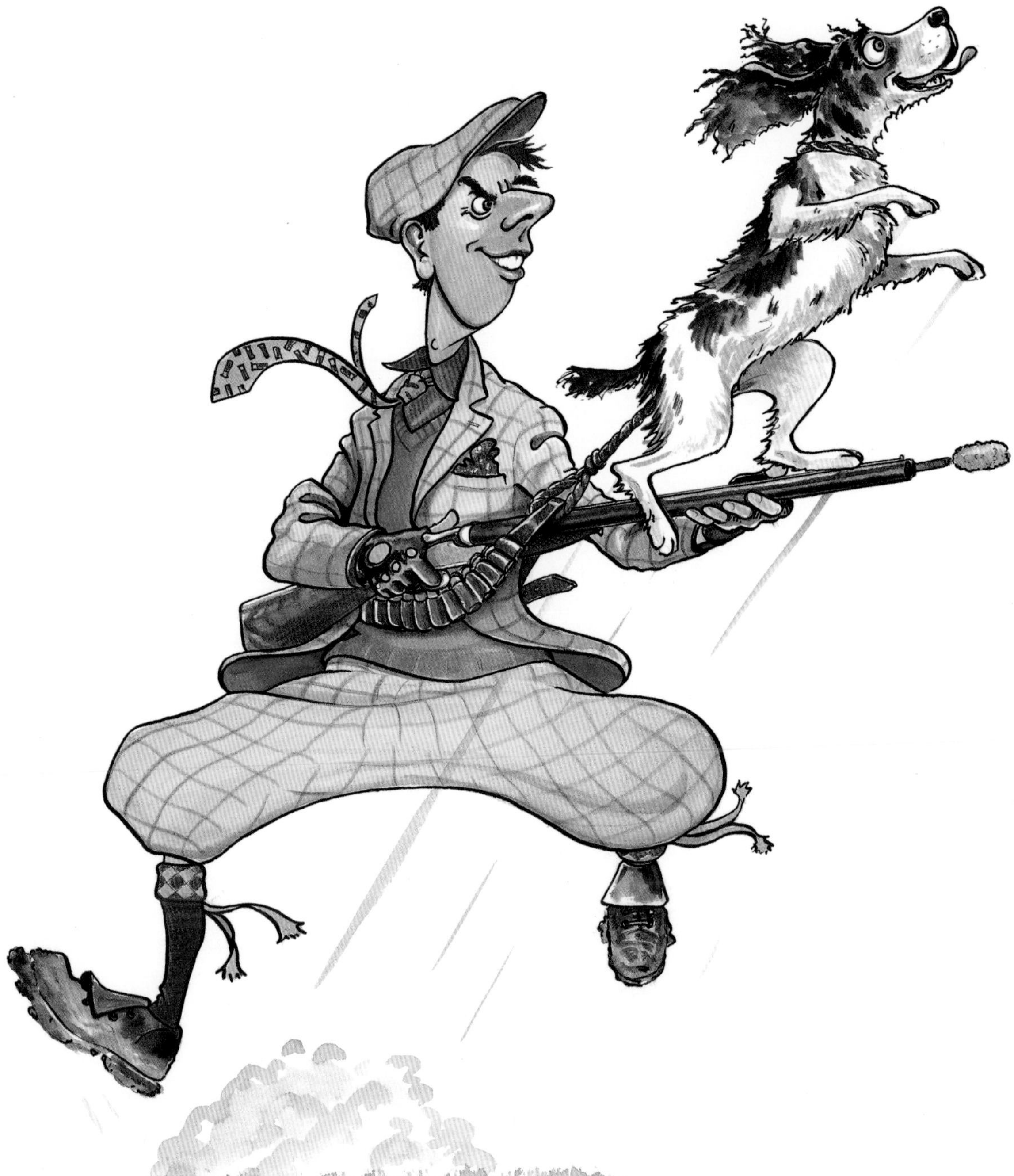

THE GRUMPY OLD BART

The bathwater ran cold. Breakfast was late, and chilly as a witch's when it did finally turn up. Without the paper, would you believe? Don't even begin to commiserate about the traffic. I mean to say, where are all these people going at this time of the morning? They should start earlier, or work nearer to home, or somewhere else. And the map was no bloody good either. Can't think whose idea that was. There should be signs. Someone should put a few up. Well, someone should be made to put a few up. Several. Lots, in fact. He has to, after all. Damn National Trust have killed almost every tree in the park, nailing signs here, there and everywhere, so the punters can find the Tea Rooms without getting lost in the gloomy interior of the front drive. Whereas he needs planning permission for a post-and-rail fence just to keep them off the croquet lawn. Unbelievable.

He only got the invitation at the last minute, couple of months ago, so he must be a second-stringer anyway. And then the gun was at the mender's because he hadn't got round to collecting it. And when he got there he was advised that he should have a thou' of these newfangled cartridges to be going on with, and the cost of those nearly delivered a seizure. Just who exactly is going to arrest him if he should pot a mallard off his own pond with a perfectly ordinary cartridge? They should try. He's been on the Bench for thirty years or more. Goes with the territory really; and he's damned if he's going to be hauled up for a spanking in front of himself for letting off lead instead of some fancy new concoction that can't be pronounced without firing your dentures across the dinner table. Dammit.

So what are we milling about here for, then? If people can't turn up on time they should be left behind. He's made it, after all, notwithstanding the horrors which are inevitably encountered the moment you set foot out of doors these days. Why can't others have the same common courtesy? Politeness of princes, that is. Not that there is much to rush for. The keeper has probably only just started blanking in the first drive. Bugger was probably still laid in bed not half an hour ago. Time was he'd have been up at first light, before, dogging in and checking on the whereabouts. Then we might have stood a chance of starting on time. As it is we will have to wait forty minutes on our pegs before a bird of some description puts in a belated appearance. Looks like rain too. Forty minutes in the freezing drizzle, just because you can't get the staff these days. Whatever happened to the work ethic?

And when the birds do pitch up, they won't be much to write home about. If he's told them once here, he's mentioned it a dozen times, they should put sewelling across the drive at the start of the plantation, then the birds won't bunch so. Like banging your head against a brick wall. They're all the same these days; a three-month course and they know it all. Mark you, the numbering has been fixed so there is little point in taking a lot of cartridges anyway. Plain as the nose on your dial. Assuming, that is, that the drives are in the usual order. Look, the middle Guns all have notable pheasant shoots which have yet to get into their main coverts, while the peripherals are the partridge men whose invitations have been enjoyed already. Cynical, *moi*? I should cocoa. Common sense.

I suppose they'll all want driving about all day too? Why can't people get their own? There'll be mud everywhere and the old trout will go ballistic when she sees the damage. Come on then, we might as well make a start. For what it's worth.

THE BLOATED PLUTOCRAT

He arrives, not in one Range Rover, but two. Or more particularly, he and his loader arrive in one, while his dogs and their handler turn up in the other. On his peg, on his shooting stick, the extra-broad hand-stitched pigskin seat squeaks comfortably against the soft, hand-woven, estate tweed–cashmere-mix-covered plutocratic bottom. The immediate vicinity is wreathed in the fragrant smoke that dribbles from the Cuban El Colossale No. 1 Super Uniquo that is clamped between perfect teeth that are both testament and advertisement for the cutting edge of modern orthodontics.

As the first carefully composed flock of birds are massaged off the runway by the keepers, his loader leans forward and murmurs a soft alert into the electronically sealed world of the Bloated Plutocrat. The European edition of the *Journal* is briskly folded and cast to the manicured sward beneath soft Schneider field-boots and the phone is tersely disconnected. One dolphin-leather-gloved hand snaps back for the birds-eye maple grip of the gilded Purdey proffered by his man. Squinting through the pink lenses of the Pengtsdorff und Schiller shades he shoots once, twice, into the densest part of the cloud. Birds tumble nearby as he reaches for his second gun and adds another brace to his mounting score. The loader dutifully clicks twice to record the event for the gold-tooled Game Book. It is illustrated with original oils by very famous artists, featuring the Bloated Plutocrat in a variety of exotic locations in the world's great helicopter-accessible wilderness, with his foot on the necks of a variety of recently deceased wildlife.

Properly satisfied with the results of his efforts, the Bloated Plutocrat subsides once more to mop his excited brow with a scented square and to take a pull of the Trafalgar brandy from his heavy silver flask. Then he centres once more the smouldering Colossale, leans forward with a murmur of silks under pressure to retrieve the *Journal* and, having restored contact once more with his man of business, he settles facing the other way to await the next drive.

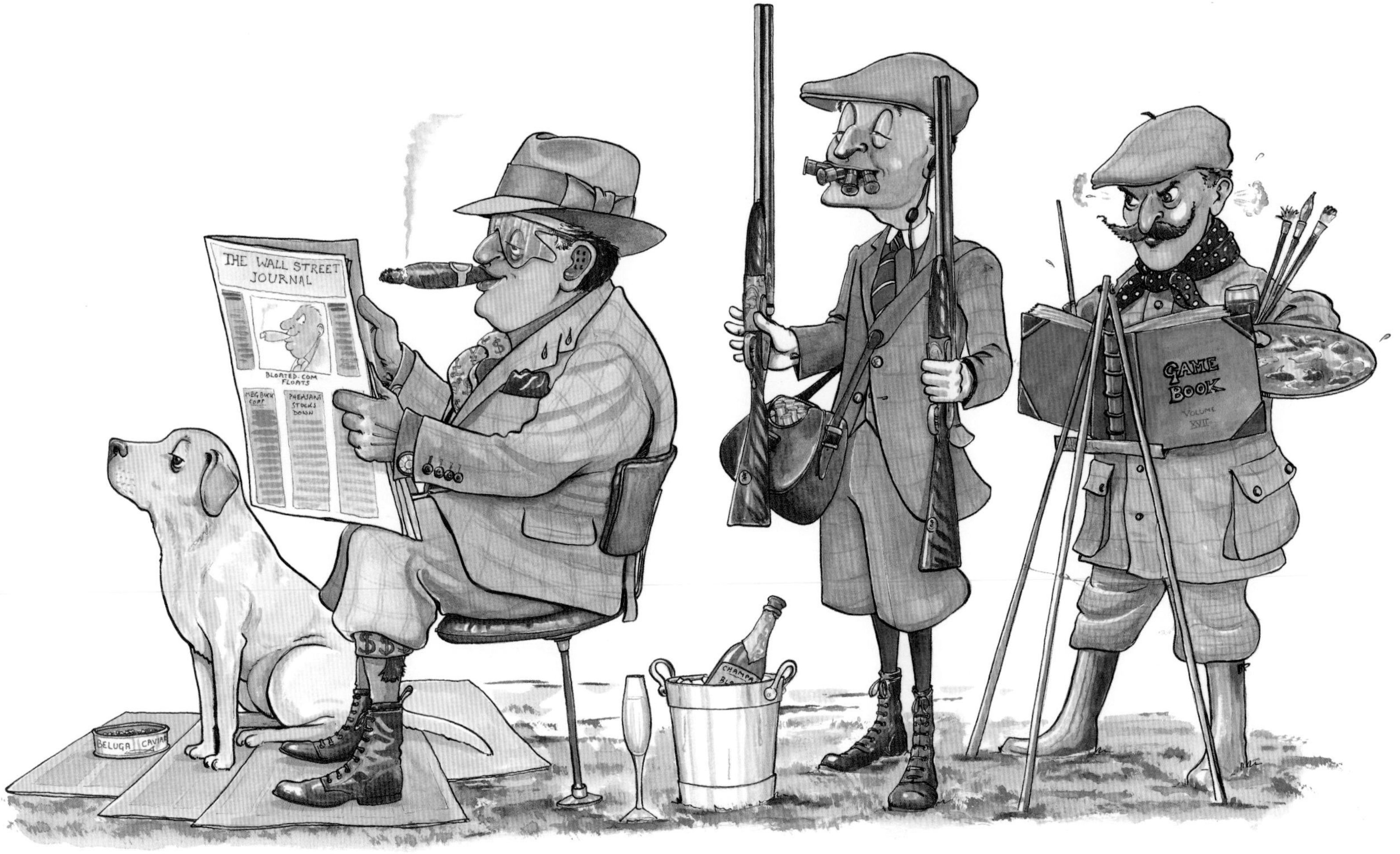
THE WALL STREET JOURNAL
BLOATED.COM FLOATS
MEGBUCK CORP
PHEASANT STOCKS DOWN
BELUGA CAVIAR
GAME BOOK
VOLUME XVII

THE YOUNG GUN

Shooting with the grown-ups for the first time. Can so much pressure ever be heaped on young shoulders? 'Be safe.' 'Be quiet.' 'Be polite.' 'Be safe.' 'Be modest.' 'Be smart.' 'Be safe.' And more 'Be's Be's', besides. A positive swarm of supercharged hormones humming about his young head, which is already spinning with excitement at the thought. There may have been lessons at Granny's knee, and walks with the keeper. There may have been outings with the old man after a pigeon and sundry armed marauds about the boundaries with the keeper, the tractor driver and Uncle Tom Cobbleigh. There may have been solitary nights in the duck hide at half term in the faint hope of an occasional bang and a mallard carried home in triumph. And lessons at the shooting school besides. But this is the first day in the line with the grown-ups. For all they are a carefully selected line of grown ups – including the aforesaid old man, sundry uncles and godfathers and a sprinkling of those friends of the folks, who are betwixt and between and who often pitch up for weekends, but who are neither blood relative nor moral guardian, and who therefore have no proper title. Too irresponsible and fun to be called Mr Whatever. Too old and aloof to be called Tom or Dick or Harry by a teenager. Let alone Pongo, Stinker or Biffy. Problems, problems, problems. Safe. Safe. Safe. Whatever you call them, there is not one who will be backward in tearing you off a strip if confronted by your muzzles across the line.

Draw for numbers like everyone else, amidst much comment about Uncle Jack and Pongo not getting a shot off between them. Stifle a blush that is already surging about the new collar like a tidal wave. Drive with Father to the first drive. He says as the engine stutters to a halt 'Just relax. And be safe.' Feel about as relaxed and safe as a bishop in a bordello, and twice as likely to go off unexpectedly. Arrive at peg and unship trusty twenty. Dump bag of shells by slip and undo coat better to reach the stiff-stiff birthday cartridge belt. Wait with cartridges in hand for the whistle before loading. Everyone is watching. Waiting for the first slip. Of course they are. They are not thinking about pheasants, or partridges, or how they might have overdone the red infuriator a bit last night, or the new girl in the office, or whether it is the nephew's birthday this week. They are all like coiled springs waiting to pounce on the first error. 'S obvious. That's why they're here.

Whistle goes; shells in. Relax. Pry fingers off fore-end. Don't click the safety like that. Fingers well away from triggers. Don't click the safety. Breathe. Occasionally. Gun is not a Black Mamba that needs strangling. Blink. 'Over! Over left!' Oh God! A pheasant. Coming. Flying. Shoot it, Uncle Jack. Pongo? Please. Yours. Mine. Oh Lord. Mount. Feet. Hands. Safety. Pull through. Blot and bang. OHMYGODDIDIGETIT?DIDI?DIDI? DIDI?

Thump.

'Nice shot,' says Uncle Jack.

'Well done,' says Pongo.

Suppress urge to gallop off to fetch bird. A flush of triumph suffuses cheeks.

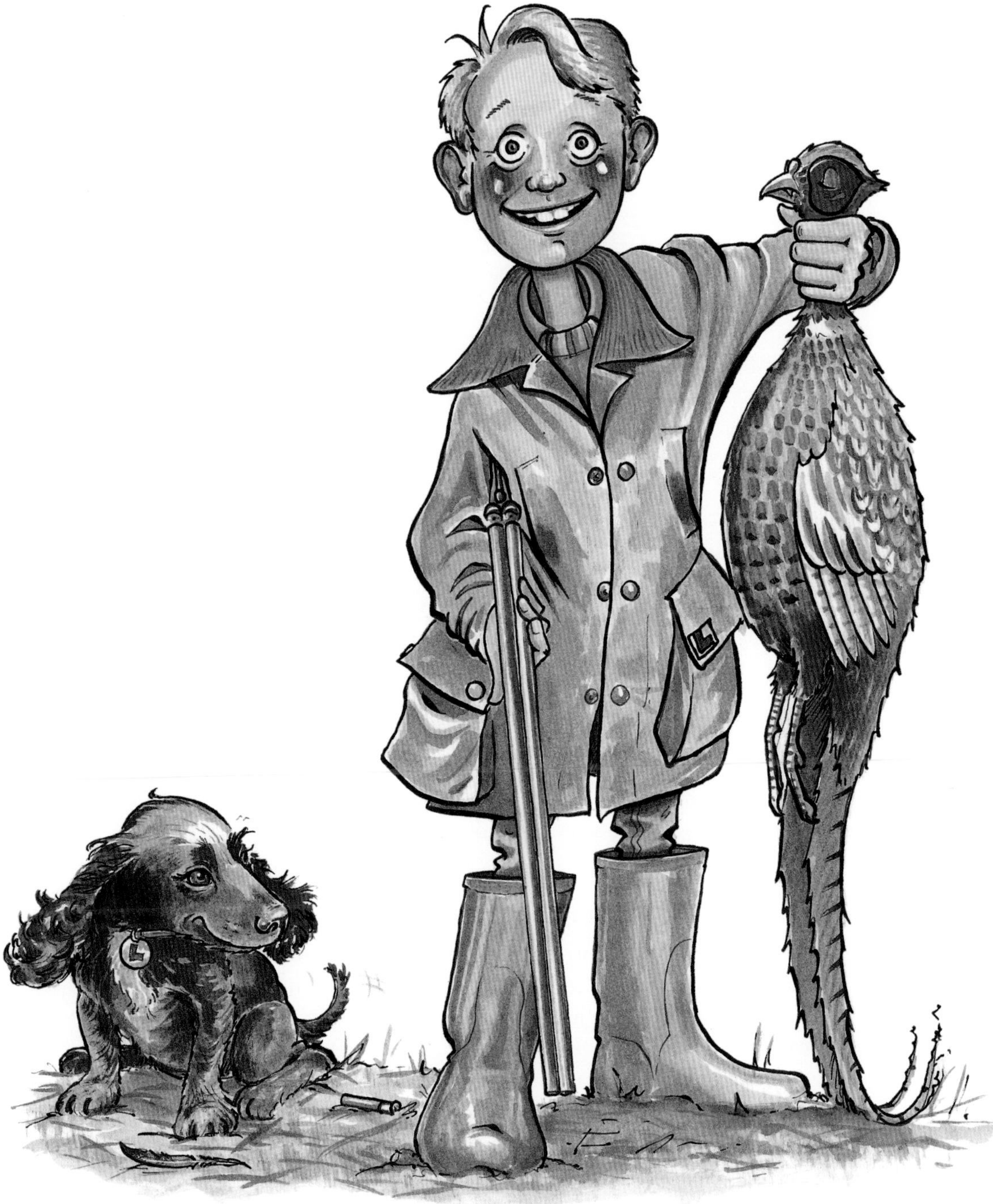

THE GREAT SHE-BEAR

She began picking up when her husband was still shooting. In those days ladies did not shoot, and to be honest she was blowed if she was going to mince about simpering all day. So she took herself off to the kennels and snagged herself a pup that no one else wanted. The pup was FTC Buckman of Swarbeam, founder of the Buckman strain, multiple winner of every prize on the circuit, saviour of babies in ponds and general all-round wonderdog, known to his close friends as 'Scrap'. Of course there will never be another like him, but one presses on regardless. She never has less than a half dozen in training, some her own and some for other people. She still has a soft spot for 'problem' dogs and there is generally one in her string which has been delivered in despair. 'Train it, keep it or shoot it' tends to be the message. Generally she keeps it, trains it, wins several championships, and parts with it for a modest fortune. 'The problem', she asserts firmly, 'is always with the owners. Hopeless, most of them. Quite hopeless.' In fact the only thing which is more hopeless than most owners is the Kennel Club, the principals of which have a special place in her considerable and descriptive vocabulary.

For the dogs, however, nothing is too good. For all she insists that they are working animals and she doesn't approve of pets, and despite the fact that they are fed on nothing more than the fallen stock which she shares with the hunt kennels, and notwithstanding that she is a lady feared as well as honoured from one end of the country to another, a glimpse of the house or the car tells a different story. There are dogs everywhere. No sofa is sacred, no bedcover unmarked. Only the kennels themselves seem not to carry the scars of extensive use by dogs. Dog hair, dog toys, dog smell, dog leads, dog dummies, dog paraphernalia, dog junk, and dogs themselves lie about the house like the fallout from so many dog bombs. Somewhere in the midst of which is the husband whose reckless comments started the whole thing off five decades ago and who has never really recovered from the shock of confronting what he let out of the bottle. He can usually be found in the study – a moderately dog-free zone – doing the crossword, practising bunker shots into the wastepaper basket and wondering how things would have turned out if he'd given her a nice set of irons as a wedding present and not suggested driving grouse as a honeymoon.

There are, for that matter, sundry children floating about. Not that it seems to matter terribly much. Given that they lived on an early diet of Bonios and were treated more or less the same as the latest batch of puppies, they haven't turned out too badly. Not Championship material, you understand, but pretty decent all-round working kids; housebroken, of course, and biddable. And dog bonkers, of course, which is all to the good. Can't imagine where they get it from.

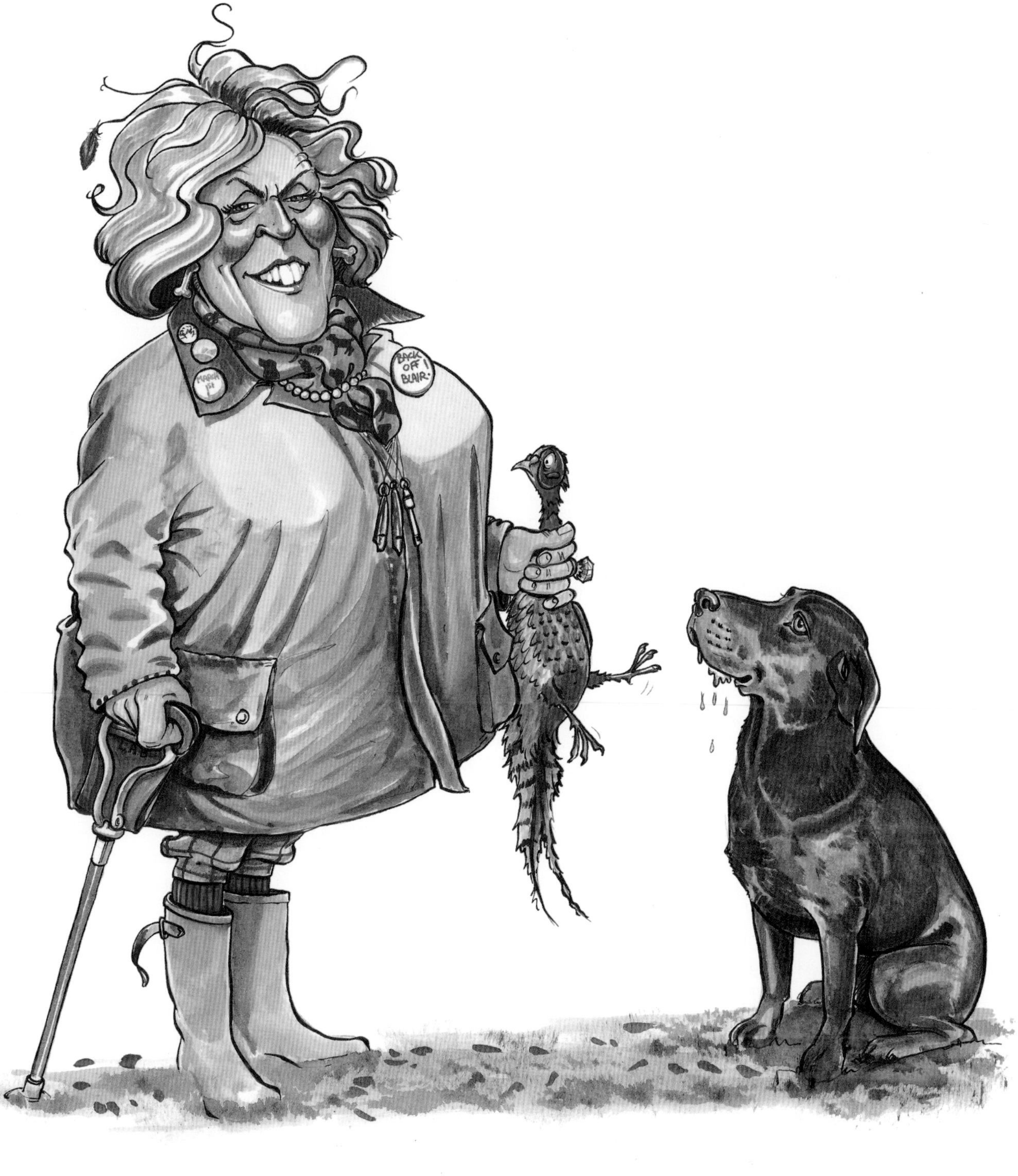
BACK OFF! BLAIR.

THE PROFESSIONAL

He arrives in a truck with a positive pack of dogs in the back; but do they teem out like lemmings as soon as the door is open? Is the Pope a Presbyterian? No, they sit in a row, bright-eyed and alert waiting for the word or the snap of the fingers that unleashes them. Sometimes only half the tide responds to the word, or as it might be, the snap; the other half staying rooted to the spot until their personal signal is given. Then they assemble in a neat semi-circle at the feet of the master.

No leads here. No choke chains or hard words. Just unquestioning, adoring obedience. Except for the pup on the one hand who has much to learn but is coming on in leaps and bounds and the oldest member of the team to whom a special licence is given to behave somewhat more like a normal dog and to seek out the smells and excitements of a shooting morning.

During a drive the team variously sit or lie behind the line, watching the shooting and marking down the birds as they fall. When a pelleted cock bounces once, gathers himself and legs it for the nearest hedge a dozen eyes flick from the bird to the boss and back again, imploring. Ooh, Sir. Me, Sir. Pleessir. Meesir. Please. 'Tess!' says the master and, like a streak of gold, or as it might be, black, Tess leaves a trail of scorched earth in her wake while the remainder stay rooted to the spot with a mixture of envy and disappointment in their expressions. Upon her return with a still-lively bird, the chosen one delivers it to hand without any of the circling or creeping of a lesser retriever. She comes, she sits, she offers up the bird and releases it without a struggle. Then she resumes her place in the row of dogs. Job done.

When the shooting is over the pup is dispatched for the dead bird nearest by. At the same time another is sent for the long bird which towered beyond the fence. 'Giddout!' and a flick of the fingers is all the direction he needs. The dog knows what he's about. And he has the trophies at home to prove it. The fence might just as well not be there as he clears it by a foot or more and is onto the bird in less time than it takes to tell. Back across the obstacle with one wing across his eyes, but that makes not a jot of difference, there is no hesitation. Then home, sit, offer up, a pat and sit down. The pup is having a problem getting the whole of her bird into her mouth. Eventually, after spitting out a couple of feathers, she gathers it up and potters somewhat tentatively back. On arrival she forgets to sit, and has her bottom grounded and is made to wait, unrelieved of her burden while another dog is sent into the lake for the bird that is floating yonder. Once he is *en route* with a spectacular flying entry, the master turns once more to the pup and relieves her of her bird and praises her extravagantly. Finally the last pair are dismissed to clear the ground of any remaining birds and then they will sweep round behind the Guns to check for birds overlooked by less diligent or skilful teams.

Can it really be like this? Always? Without fail? Where are the japes, the antics, the tantrums and the plain bloody-mindedness that inform the relationships of the rest of us with our dogs? In the past is where. In the past. Amateurs have anecdotes, professionals have prizes. That's the difference.

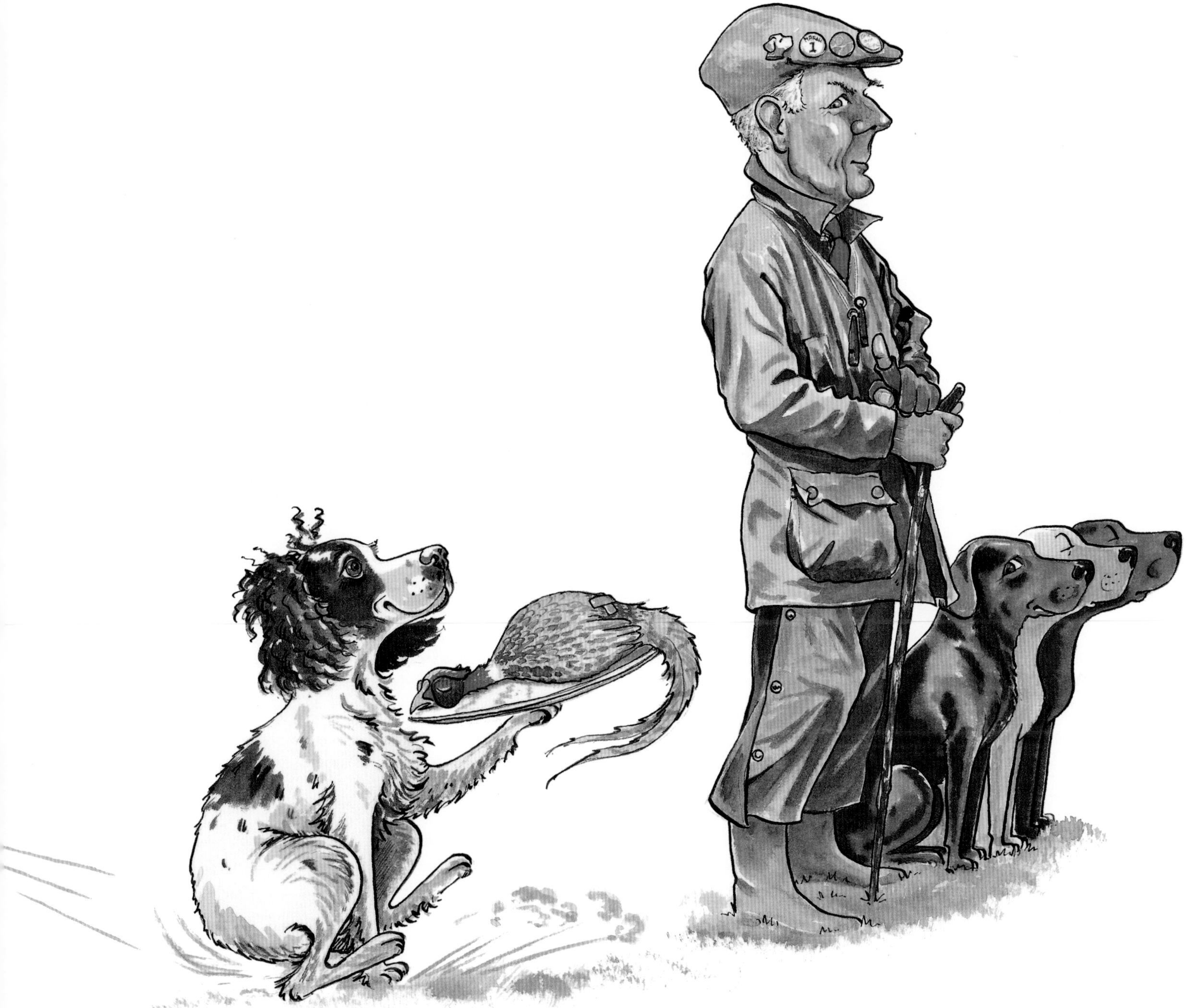

THE WILDFOWLER

Instantly recognisable by the fact that he is utterly unrecognisable. From the balaclava helmet underneath the Russian fur hat at one end, through the pneumatic vastness of well-padded waterproofs in the middle to the colossal waders at the bottom end, the wildfowler is uniformly clad in mud. Not merely mud-coloured, but actual mud. And not just any old mud, such as you might pick up in a field in which, through oversight, you skidded or indeed a ditch into which one might inopportunely plummet; but mud such as is found only in the most remote regions of these isles and then a little way beyond that.

For the wildfowler's domain lies below the high-water mark, and whether it be coast, estuary, river or mere, it is out on the flats, beyond the creeks or below the banks that the best mud can be found, for there be fowl. And not just any old fowl either. You or I might account for the occasional mallard during a shooting day, or even a teal, but the wildfowler is after wilder game. Wigeon, Garganey, Pochard and Gadwall. Golden-eye and Scoter (velvet as well as Common), Scaup, Pintail and Shoveller. Plover, Godwit and Redshank. And the geese of course, Whitefront, Pinkfoot, Grey-leg, and Bluish under the armpit. No, you're right, the last one was made up. Nonetheless the wildfowler is able to distinguish between each of these and confidently raises his gun to each and all – in the dark. For the final feature of wildfowling is that it must be undertaken largely in the middle of the night. And with the biggest guns that may conveniently be lugged the great distances involved and let off without sustaining serious, too serious, injury.

Thus when the rest of us are returning from a day in the field, the wildfowler is packing for the journey. All through the night he drives to some far-flung and remote spot unpolluted by mortal men – other than wildfowlers. Here he envelops himself in many layers of vests and woolly underthings, covered in many more layers of shirtings and woolly overthings, topped off with an impermeable layer of rubber and muddy outerthings. Then he grasps his great double 8-bore to his bosom and strides off into the dark to find some decent mud. Once having discovered, by virtue of falling into several, a likely looking – or more probably feeling – salting, creek or dyke, the wildfowler embeds himself in its comfortable mud and waits for dawn or the tide; whichever arrives first.

If it is the dawn he waits some more until the fowl begin to move. This they do in wide circles around those ditches and creeks which are inhabited by fowlers. After an hour or so the fowler becomes sufficiently frustrated that he lets off his great gun anyway and begins to stumble home. At which point the tide arrives. Cut off from any effective route back to civilisation by the rising waters, the wildfowler spends the next four hours until the tide begins to ebb perched atop a muddy island taking comfort from the bleakness of his surroundings and solace from the howling of the wind. If the tide rises further, the fowler sits tight, dismantles his gun and uses the barrels as a snorkel until the water goes down. For this reason 8-bores always have three-foot barrels, giving rise to the expression 'going the last yard'.

Wildfowlers disdain other shooters because of the vastness of their bags, and venerate Sir Peter Hawker because he was the last wildfowler who actually shot something.

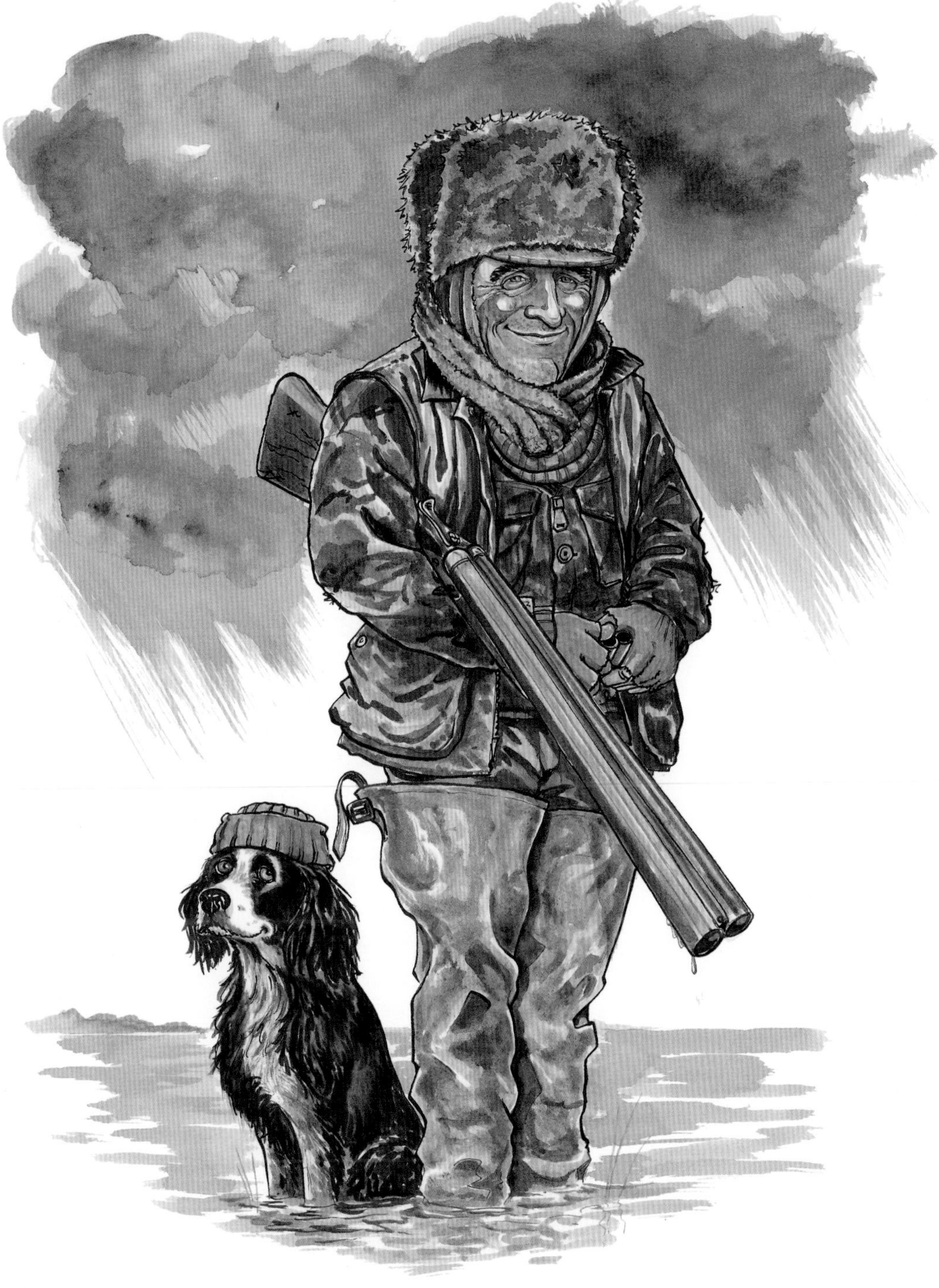

THE EUROSHOT

Like an October pheasant floundering over the wire of the release pen, the Euroshot is a target unworthy of a true sportsman. So here goes. Shaving-gear in the hatband, obsessed with the size of his trophy and a predilection for arriving in the field in what can only be described as suede hot pants. And that's only the northerners. Moving steadily south, or downhill as it is sometimes described, and we encounter aftershave, smarm and garlic, all in industrial quantities. They mangle the language, seduce the staff and execute the livestock. And then they buy our gunmakers. The bounders have zips in their wellingtons, for heaven's sake. And look confused when you explain who invented them.

Mark you, they are as nothing compared to your actual Mediterraneans. Over and unders, shoot anything that moves – and most things that don't. Drink like fish – from the bottle – sleep all afternoon and can't be trusted with donkeys. They pee in the garden, flounce about draped in lambswool pullies, have gold teeth, no morals and tend to disappear when the bill arrives. They are low, sleek, garish, fast, thirsty and unreliable; just like their lousy sports cars. And to crown it all they have this universal tendency at the end of the day, when the meagre bag is laid out on the lawn – two starlings, a Gloucester Old Spot, three pheasants, eight rabbits and the under-gardener – of setting fire to the hedge and playing a trumpet voluntary in honour of the dear departed. Well, really. It's just too easy and we should not go down that road, however much fun it is.

The Germans contribute significantly to the maintenance of the place in Scotland, while the Belgians and the Dutch consistently prop up the prices of agricultural land in East Anglia, which they largely built – or salvaged – in any event. The French bring their own claret and a stream of unfeasibly pretty girlfriends; while the Spanish have provided everybody for a generation with his first 20-bore. And the Italians, if we are good, will let us have a go in the two-seater as well as making the only over and unders which don't look like agricultural machinery. And while we are on the candour jag, we ourselves are a bunch of bulky, red-faced individuals who tend to have a good deal of breakfast, and dinner for that matter, smeared across our waistcoats. We wear inherited trousers the size of zeppelins, live in abject poverty in freezing-cold houses where we engage in unnatural practices learned when our mad parents abandoned us, aged nine, on the steps of some Gothic workhouse. And whenever someone is named Tom or Dick or Harry, we insist, for no particular reason that anyone can remember, on calling them Stinks, Bunny and Pongo.

We are all Europeans now, I'm told. So there.

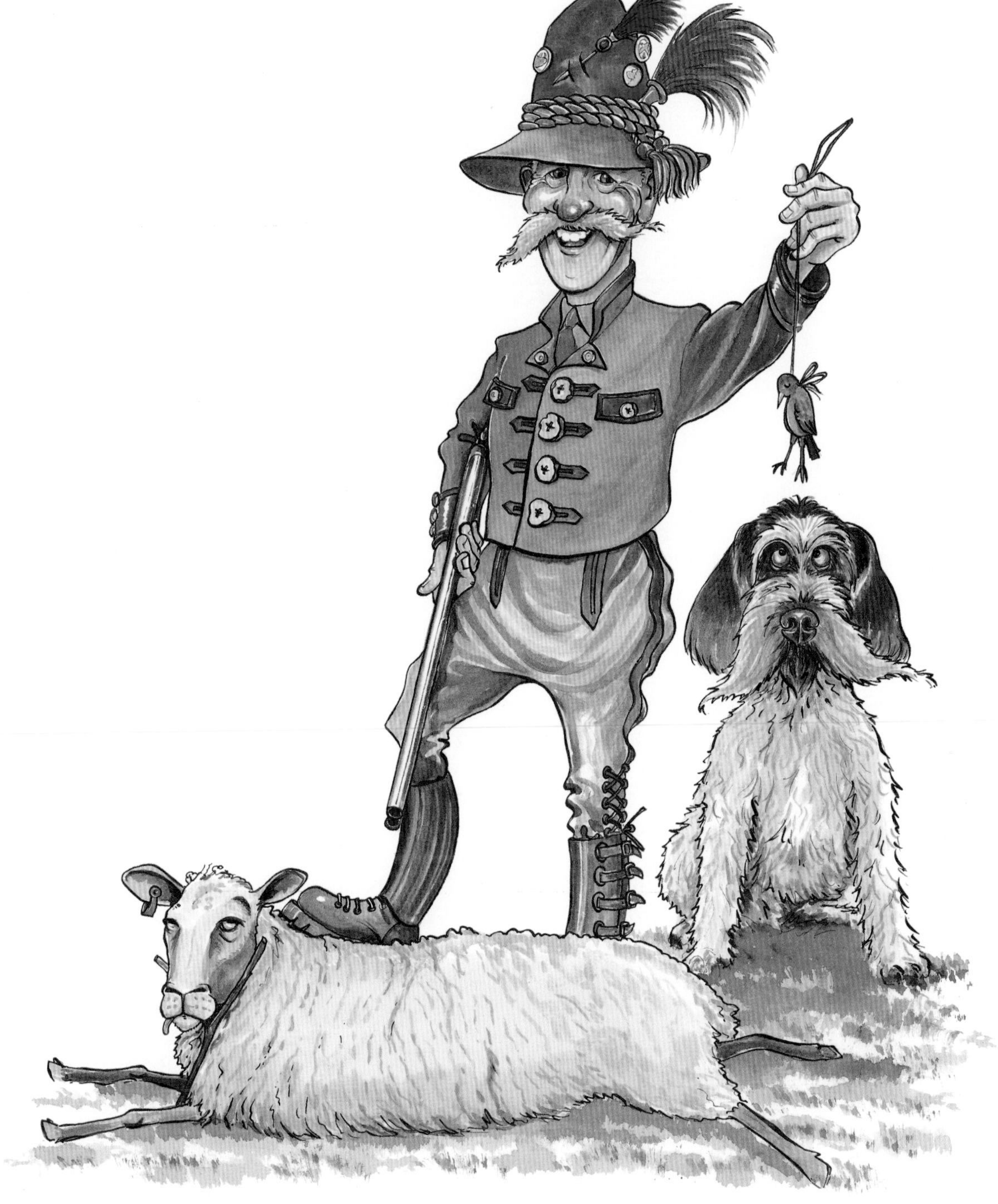

THE HIGH-PHEASANT SPECIALIST

Thirty-four-inch barrels, ported by Mag-Na-Port. Full and full, natch. Monte Carlo stock and single trigger, of course, and the whole thing weighs nearer eight pounds than seven. Basically a trap gun with a comb so high it'll have your eye out; for all it is handcrafted in Gardone by the finest Italian craftsmen and costs a small, scratch that, a large fortune. Slap a 'scope on the top and it would be a rifle. But when you are shoving 1¼ oz of nickel-plated Hi-Powa Dynamite Dobermanns in the other end you need some bulk to absorb the repercussions when the action starts. Try a couple of boxes of these total headbangers yourself in short order when you have half an hour to spare and suddenly the slightly vacant and faraway expression of the High-Pheasant Specialist begins to make sense.

And what is the objective of this pain and anguish? To shoot pheasants which are a very long way away indeed. Not fast pheasants necessarily, like they have out on the Fens, or the wild unruly pheasants that hurtle cackling from the bracken beds of East Anglia or corkscrew through the branches of the hanging woods of Yorkshire. These are perfectly ordinary pheasants launched off vertiginous escarpments which plummet towards the distant valley floor where, like an ant at the foot of a dry well, stands the High-Pheasant Specialist. The drives are called K2, or Cumulo Nimbus or perhaps The Outer Rings of Saturn. Like cars called The Senator or Grande Luxe or Tankbuster, the names seek by inference to raise the perceived quality of these unfortunate birds to somewhere above and beyond the mere quarry that the rest of us pursue. And to justify the truly sky-high amounts of money with which the High-Pheasant Specialist parts in order to let off his gun many times down a deep hole.

There once was a man who stood in his garden in the heart of the city and let off his gun many times. A policeman arrived and enquired of the citizen what he was about. 'I'm shooting the famous high pheasants of the West Country,' said he, 'It's rare sport and no mistake.' The bobby scratched his bonce, bemused; 'But we are hundreds of miles from the West Country.' 'Aye,' said the shooter, with a wink, 'they may not actually be very high, but they surely are a bloody long way away!'

THE PIGEON SHOOTER

Swathed from head to foot in the last word in Cammo, it is sometimes hard to tell the pigeon shooter from the tree. Out on the stubbles, however, he stands out like the proverbial rugby ball on a billiards table. And there is the noise, of course, since his every movement is accompanied by the sound of a mighty rushing wind as various layers of man-made fibre abrade one another and create a lightning storm of static.

Crouched in a ditch or under a hedge or lurking at the foot of a long wood, the pigeon shooter diligently sets out his stall. Decoys are dangled in the trees above, planted out on the crop in front and set about, head to wind obviously, to attract the passing traffic. Feeders, wobblers and bobbers are variously pegged, pinned and inflated and merry-go-rounds, gliders and flappers are set up and powered by strings attached to the pigeon shooter's outlying limbs, or by cables attached to car batteries and small portable generators.

The hide is then constructed by hammering a series of modest girders into the ground at intervals, from which is suspended several more yards of camouflage netting and against which are set a selection of branches, twigs, leaves, fertiliser bags, tractor tyres and sundry parts of a Cortina in order to accurately recreate the proper look of an average hedge. Inside, the pigeon shooter ensconces himself on a collapsible chair with his binoculars, a short-wave radio for communication with base, a portable radar screen and a sack of cartridges close to hand, and avails himself of the large flask or canteen which will sustain him through the afternoon.

The pigeons, meanwhile, are gathered for a meeting round the gas gun on the far side of the Old Sixty Acre. From time to time one of them will clap by the pigeon shooter just to see if he is ready yet to be persuaded to lug his gear to the other end of the field. Or whether he still harbours hopes of a record bag. When these occasional observers find themselves sidestepping the odd desperate shot at eighty yards out and more they know that they have another Cammo scalp for their sitty tree.

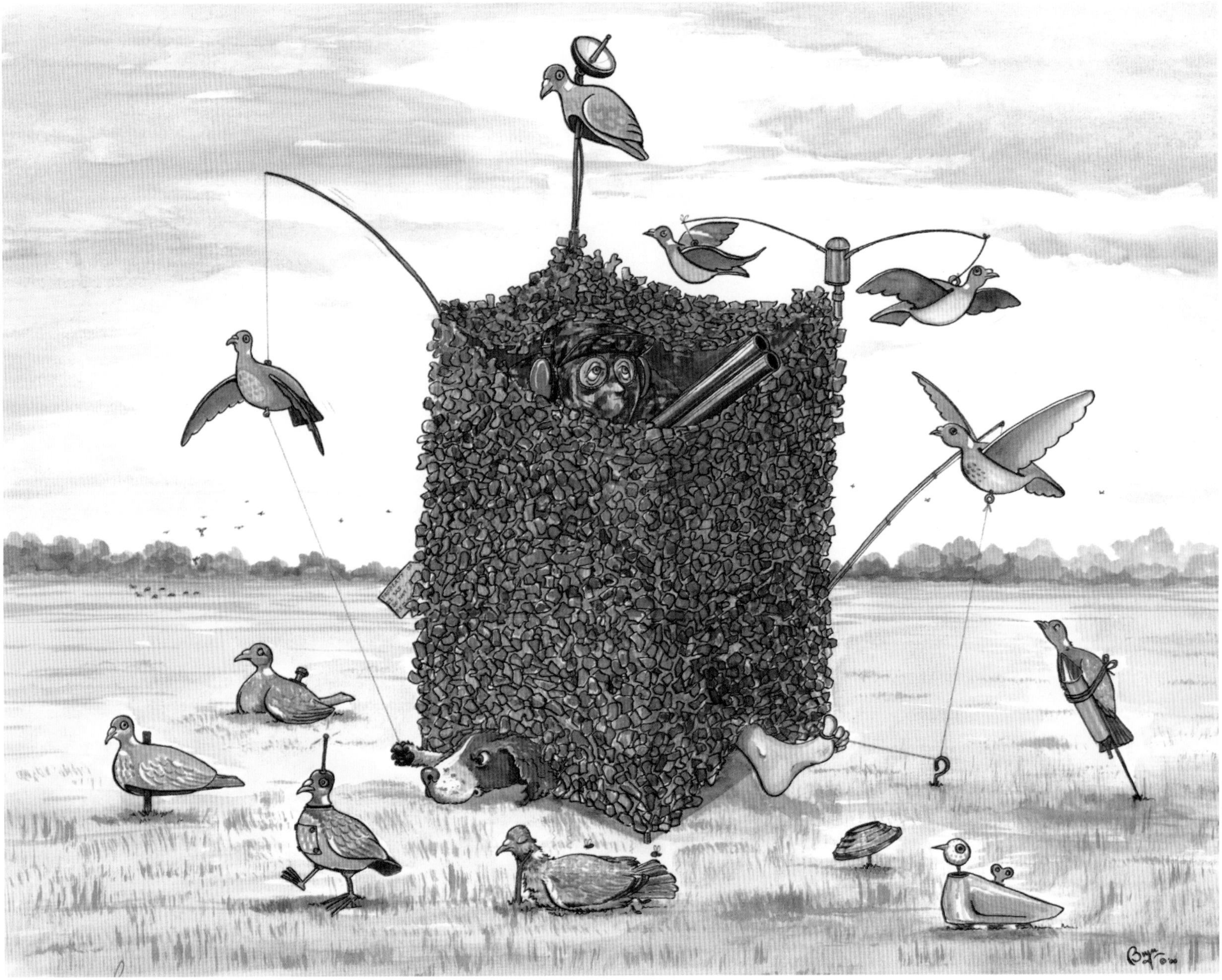

CHAPTER 4

The Quarry

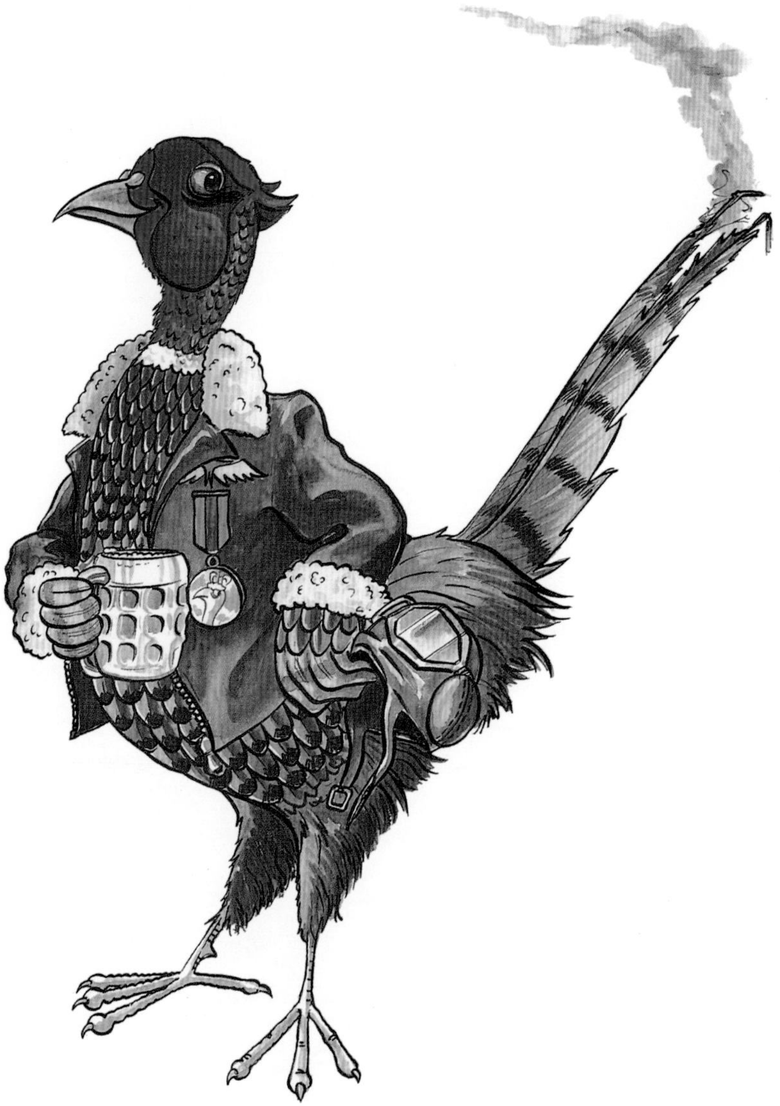

THE VETERAN

ENGLISH PARTRIDGE

FRENCH PARTRIDGE

LAME DUCK

INFAMOUS GROUSE

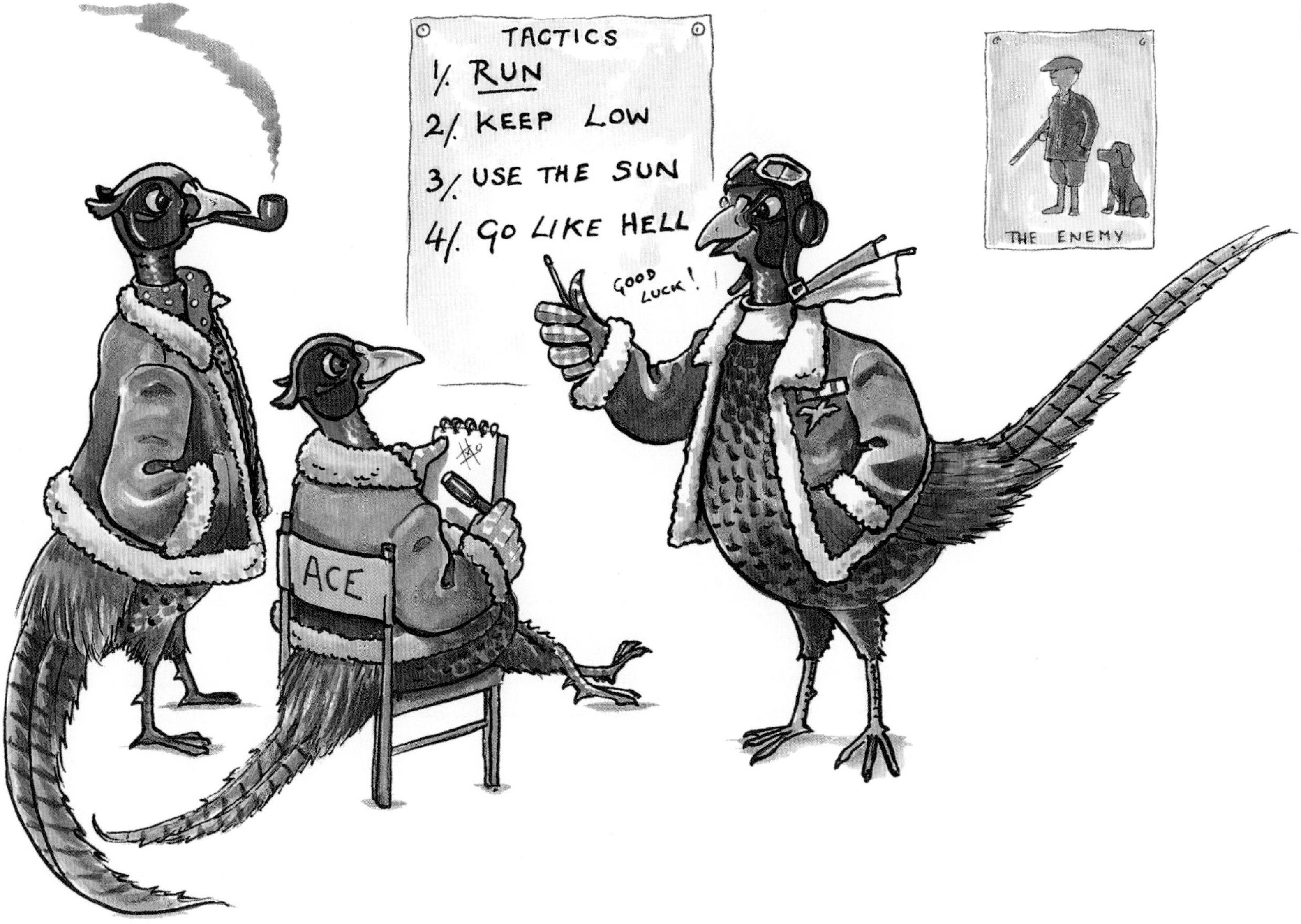
TACTICS
1/. RUN
2/. KEEP LOW
3/. USE THE SUN
4/. GO LIKE HELL
GOOD LUCK!
THE ENEMY
ACE

Open Season . . . . .

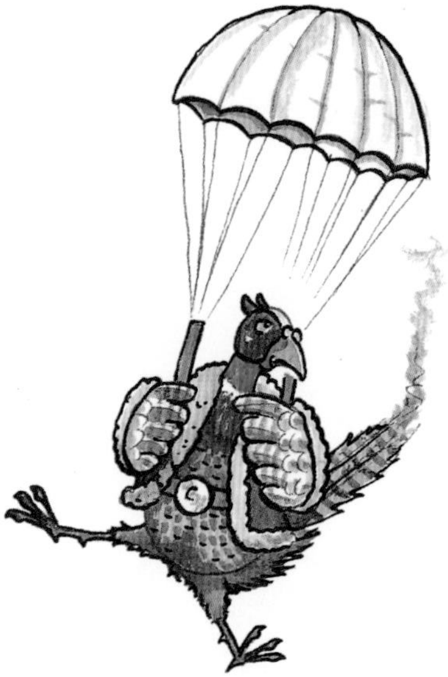

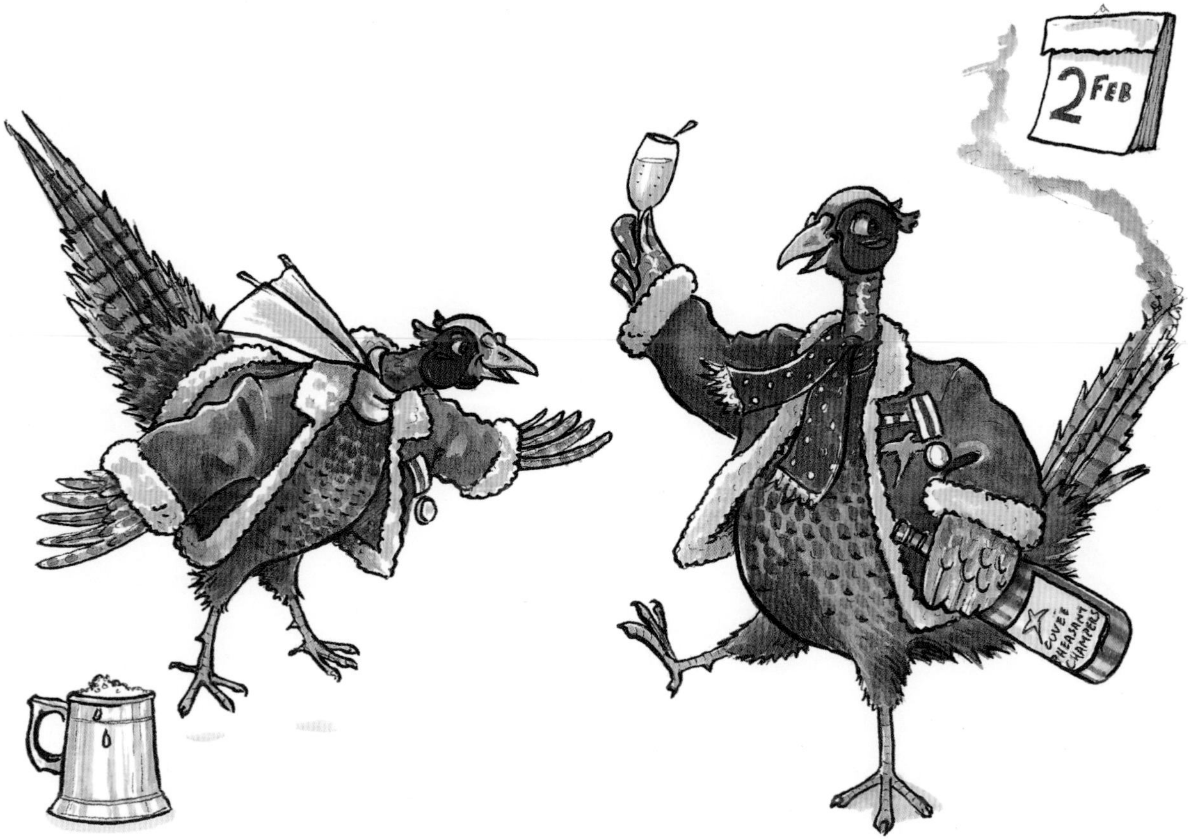
2 FEB

. . . . . CLOSE SEASON

Training for Perfection

Perfect Partners

TRAINING WITH THE DUMMY

TRAINING TO THE WHISTLE

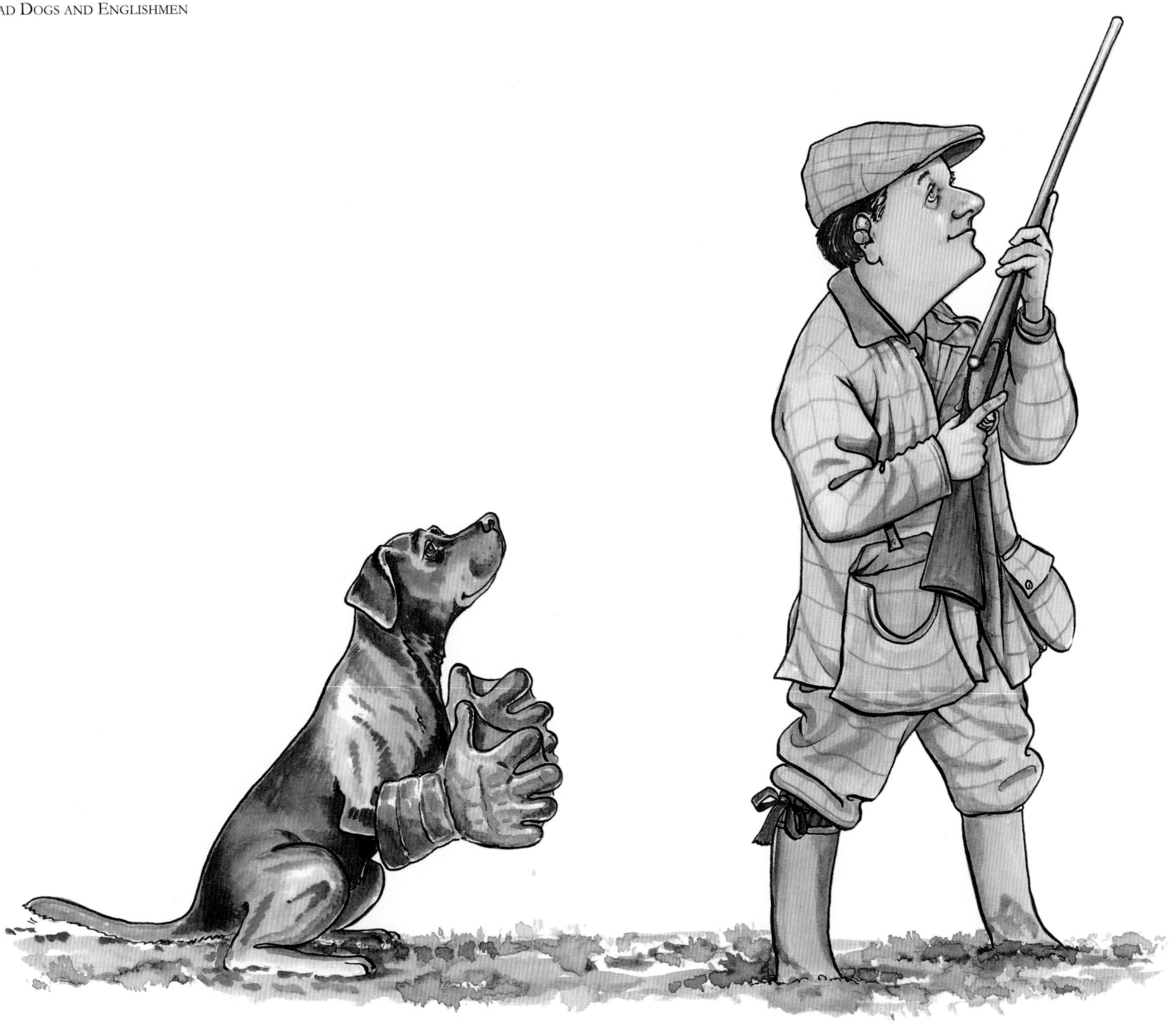

Over!

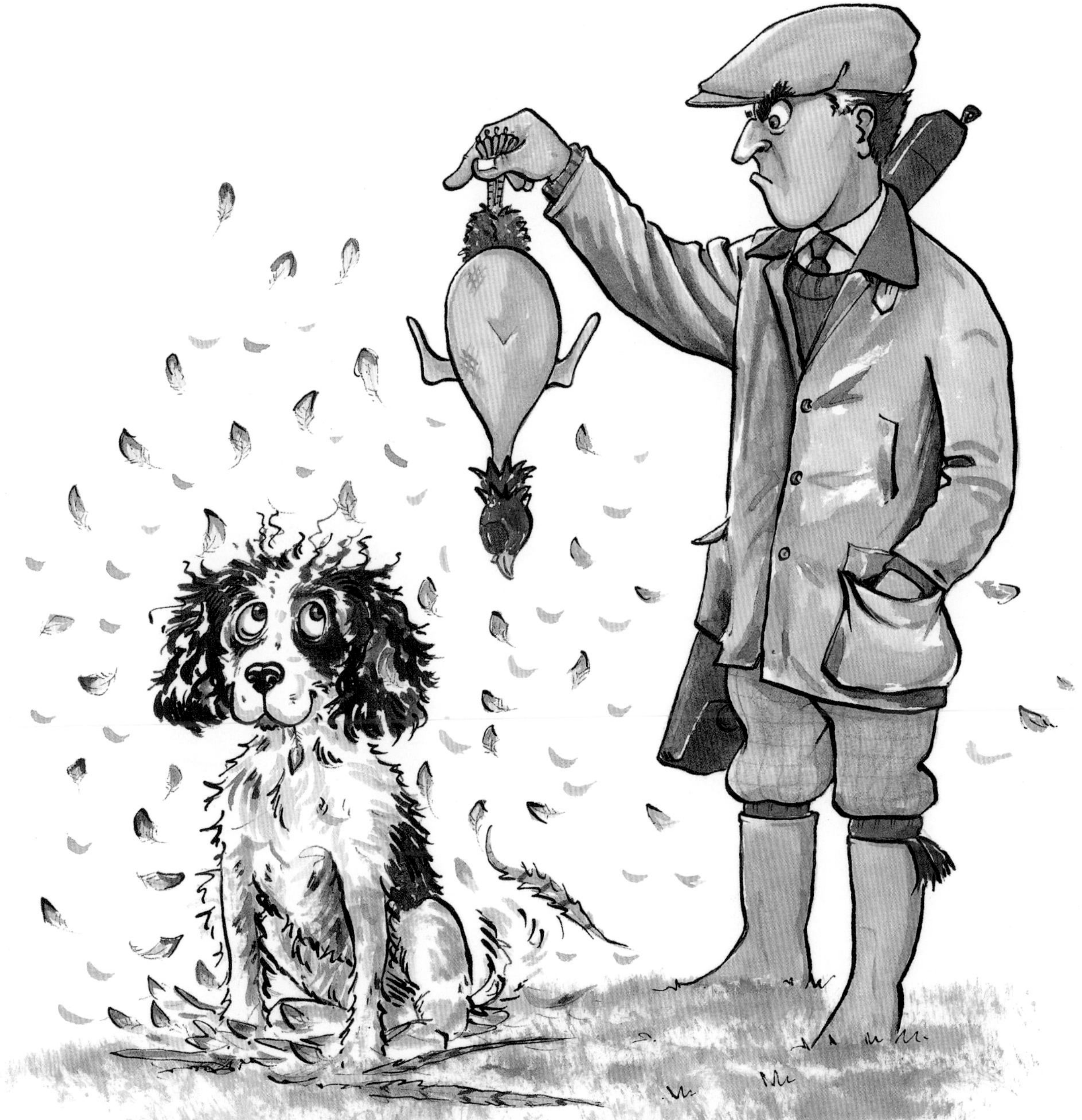

Oven Ready

THE RUNNER

SWINGING THROUGH

THE RELUCTANT PARTICIPANT

THE FAITHFUL RETRIEVER

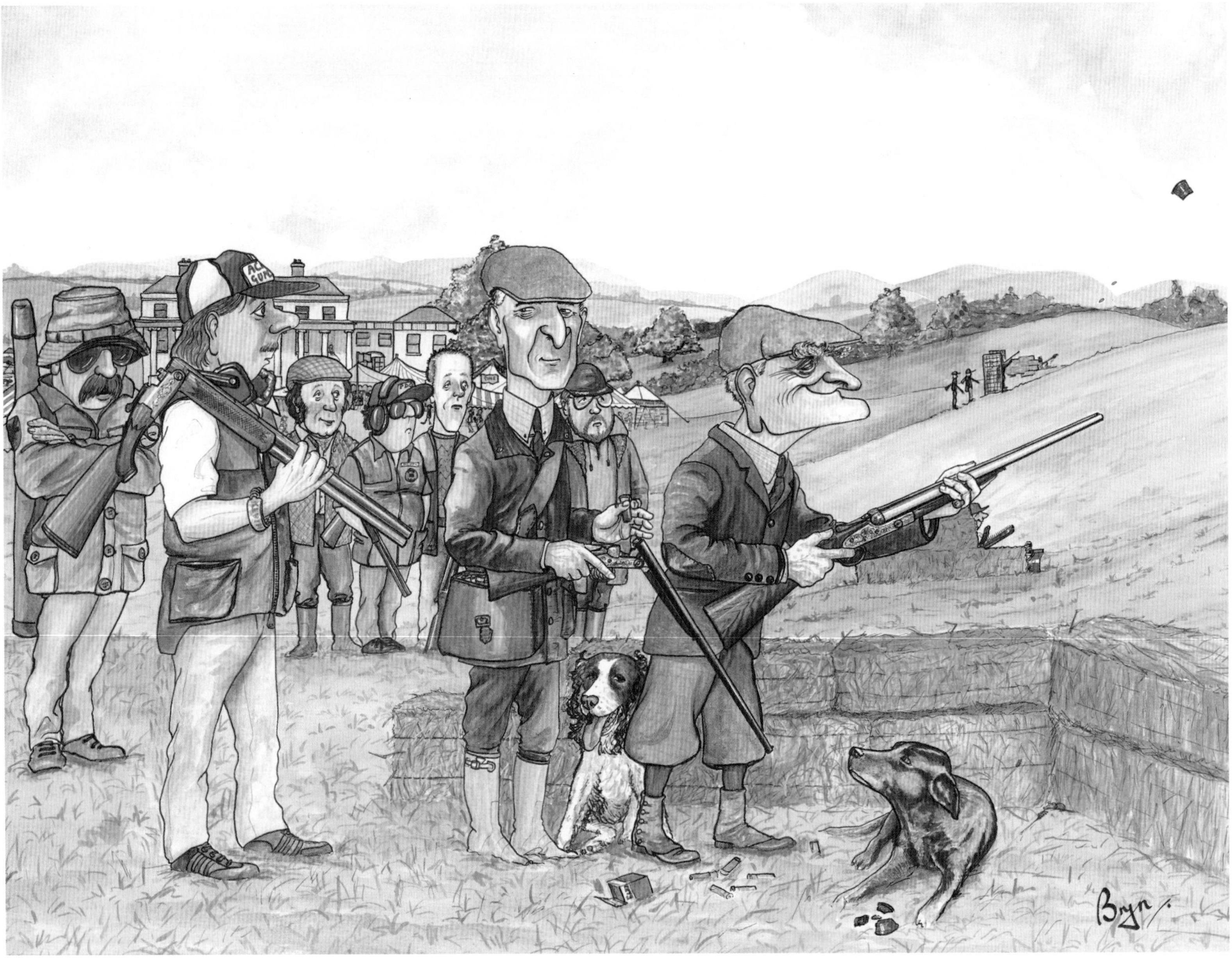
Bryn

The Old Gun

CHAPTER 6

Into the Field

ANOTHER PERFECT DAY

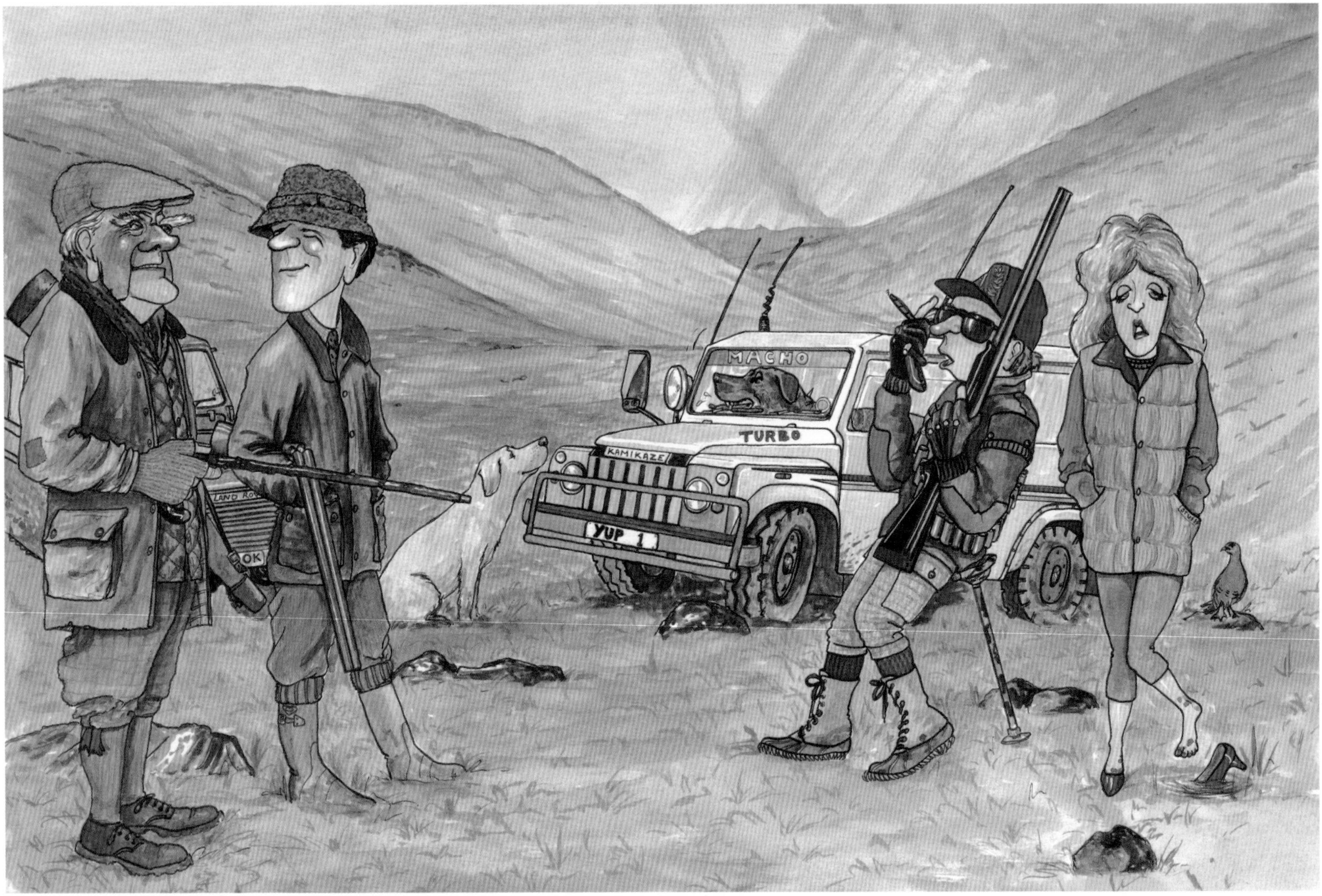
MACHO
TURBO
KAMIKAZE
YUP 1
OK

Kamikaze Macho Turbo

SAFETY FIRST

'IT SEEMED A SHAME TO CANCEL WHEN WE ALL ENJOY IT SO'

'I THINK IT'S STARTING TO BRIGHTEN UP, DON'T YOU?'

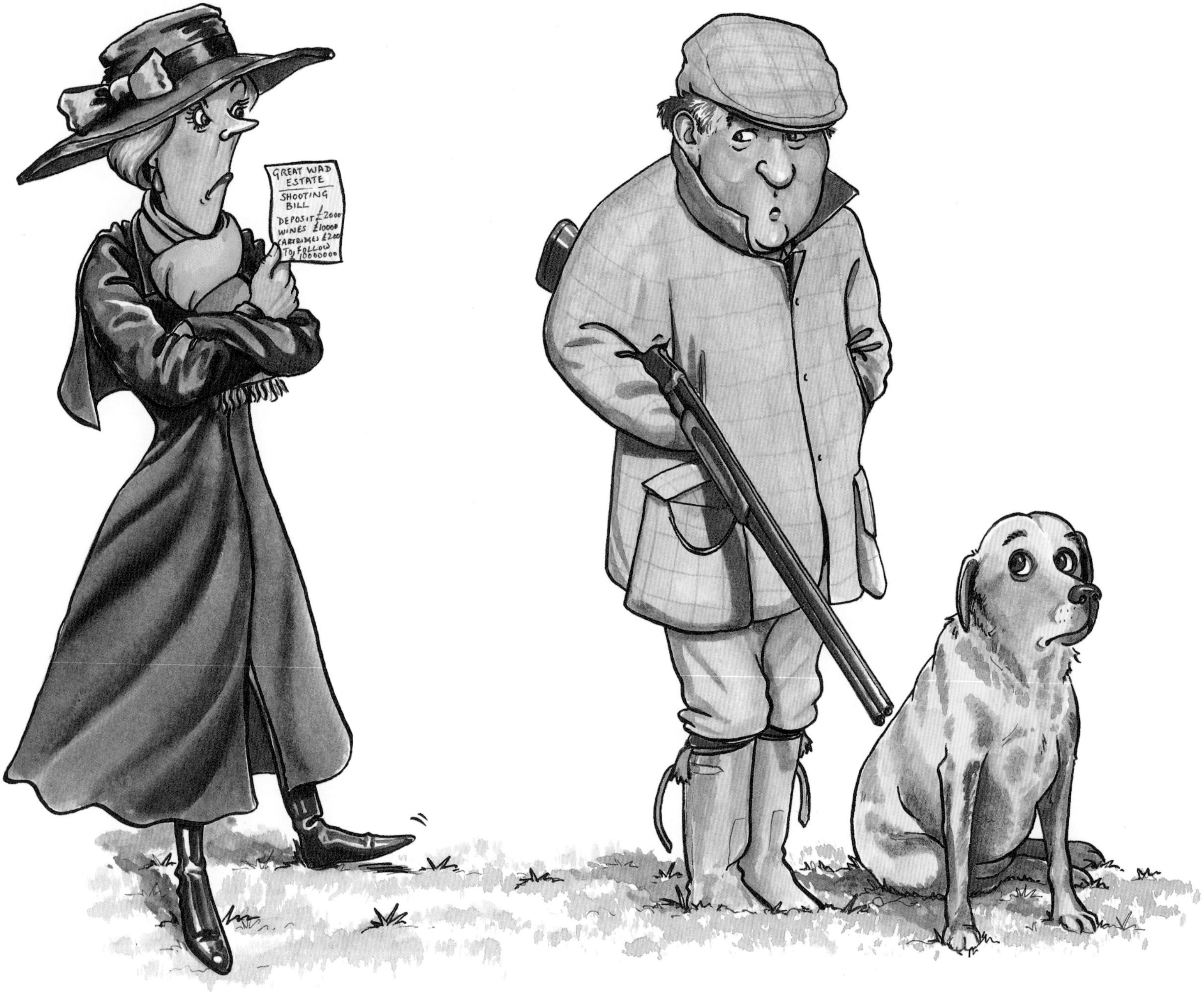
GREAT WAD ESTATE
SHOOTING BILL
DEPOSIT £2000
WINES £10000
CARTRIDGES £200
TO FOLLOW £10000000

The Shoot Bill

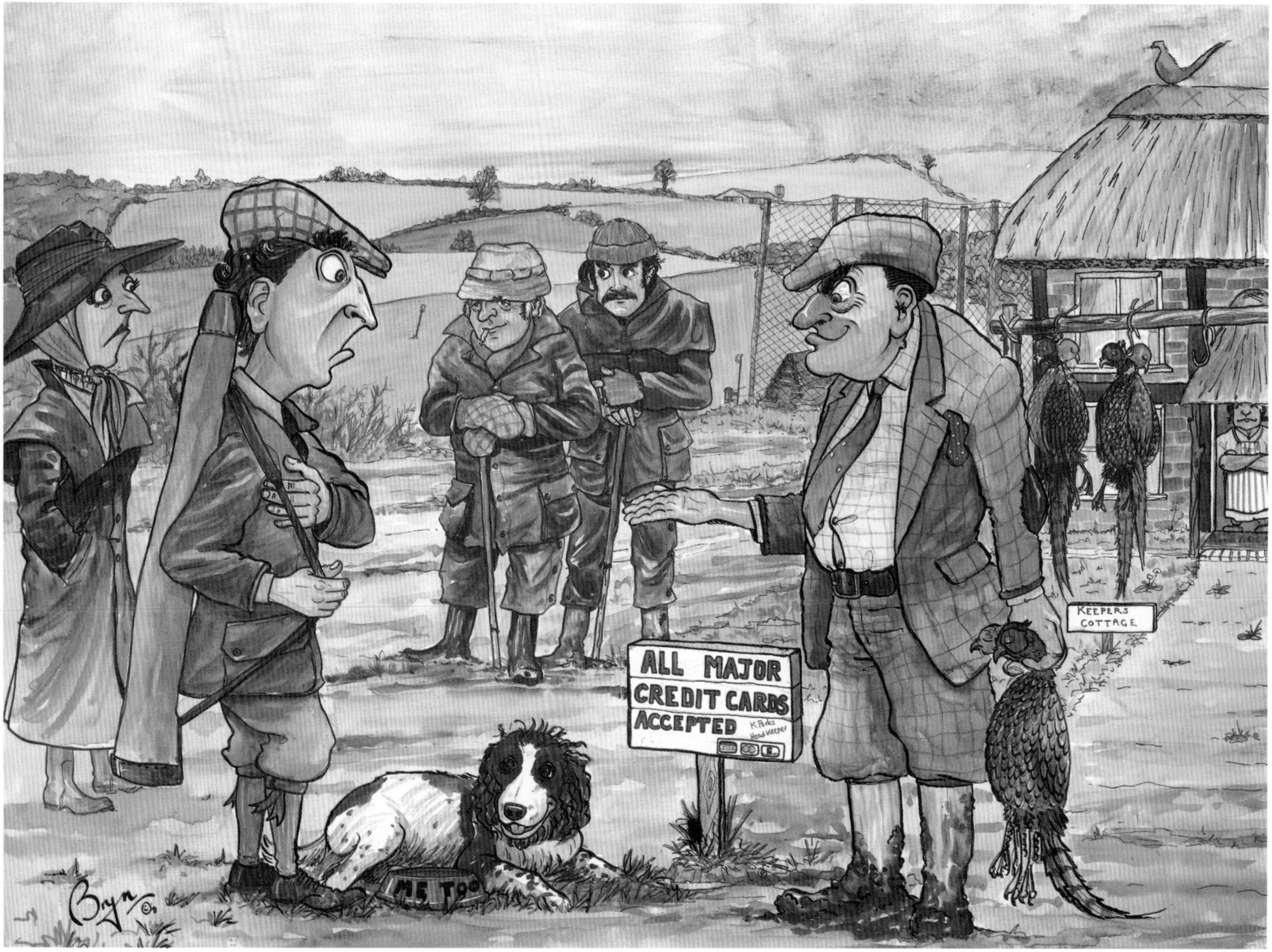
ALL MAJOR
CREDIT CARDS
ACCEPTED
K.Perks
Head Keeper
KEEPERS
COTTAGE
MS TOO
Bryn

The Keeper's Tip

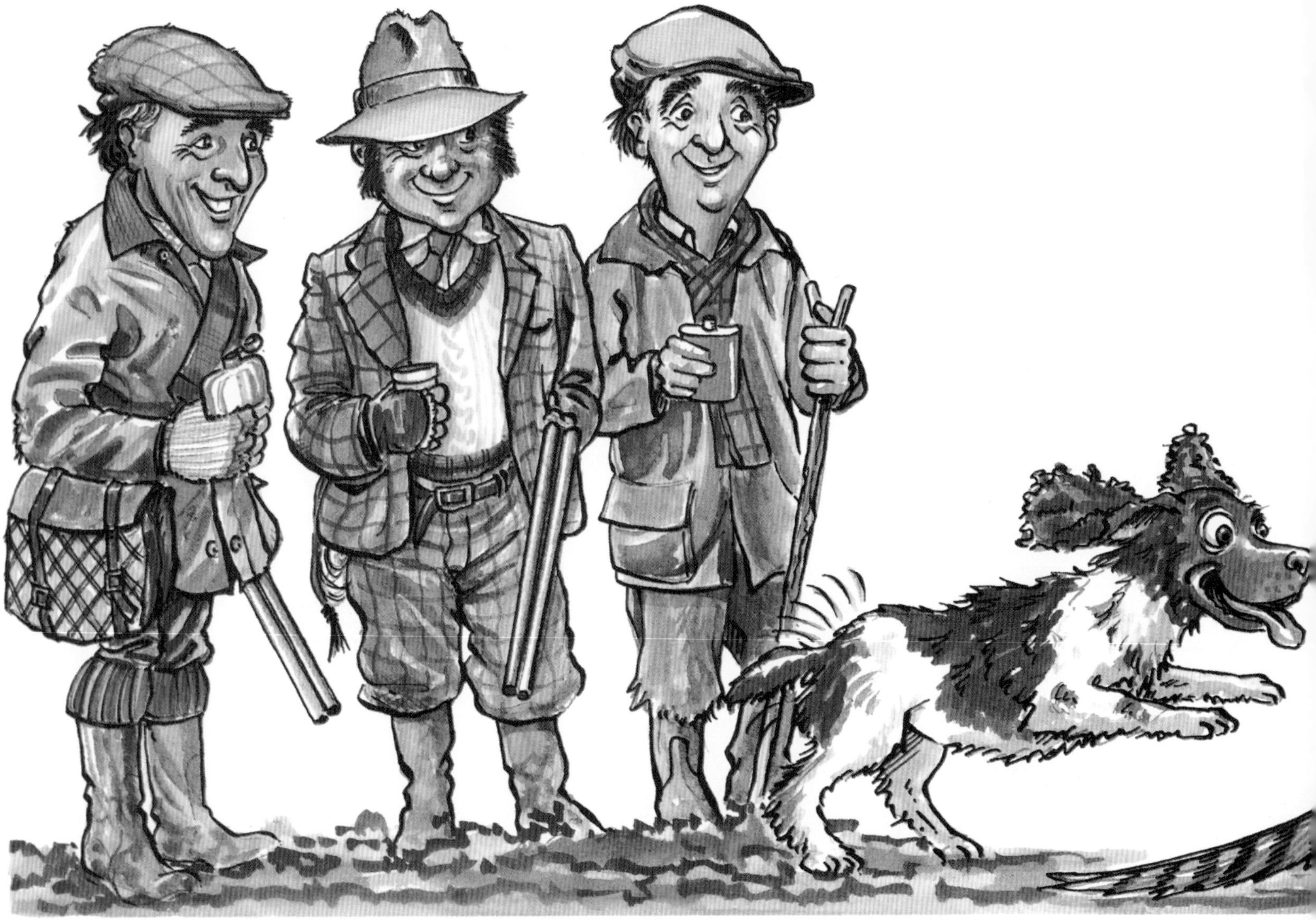

Fun Shoot . . . . .

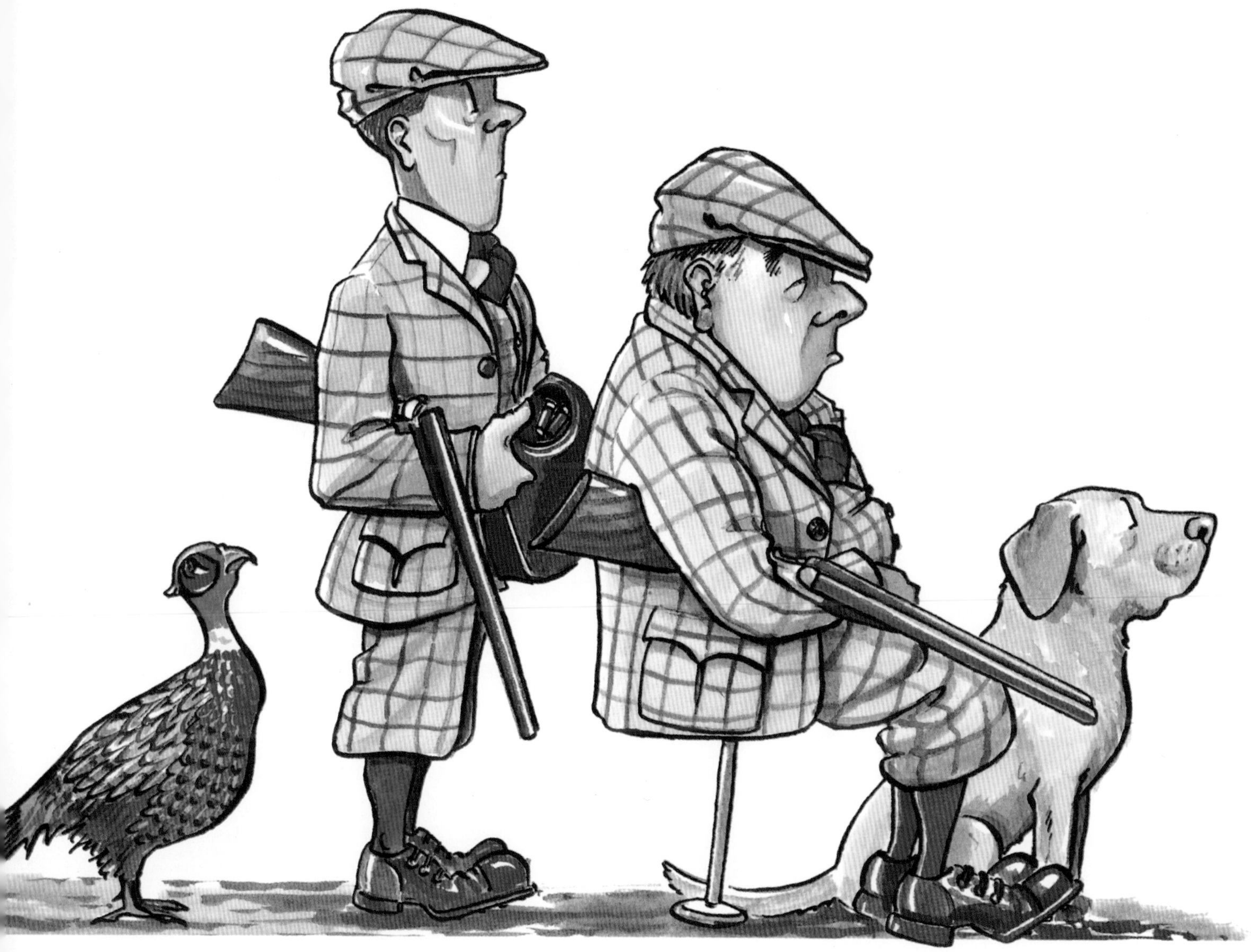

. . . . . Serious Shoot

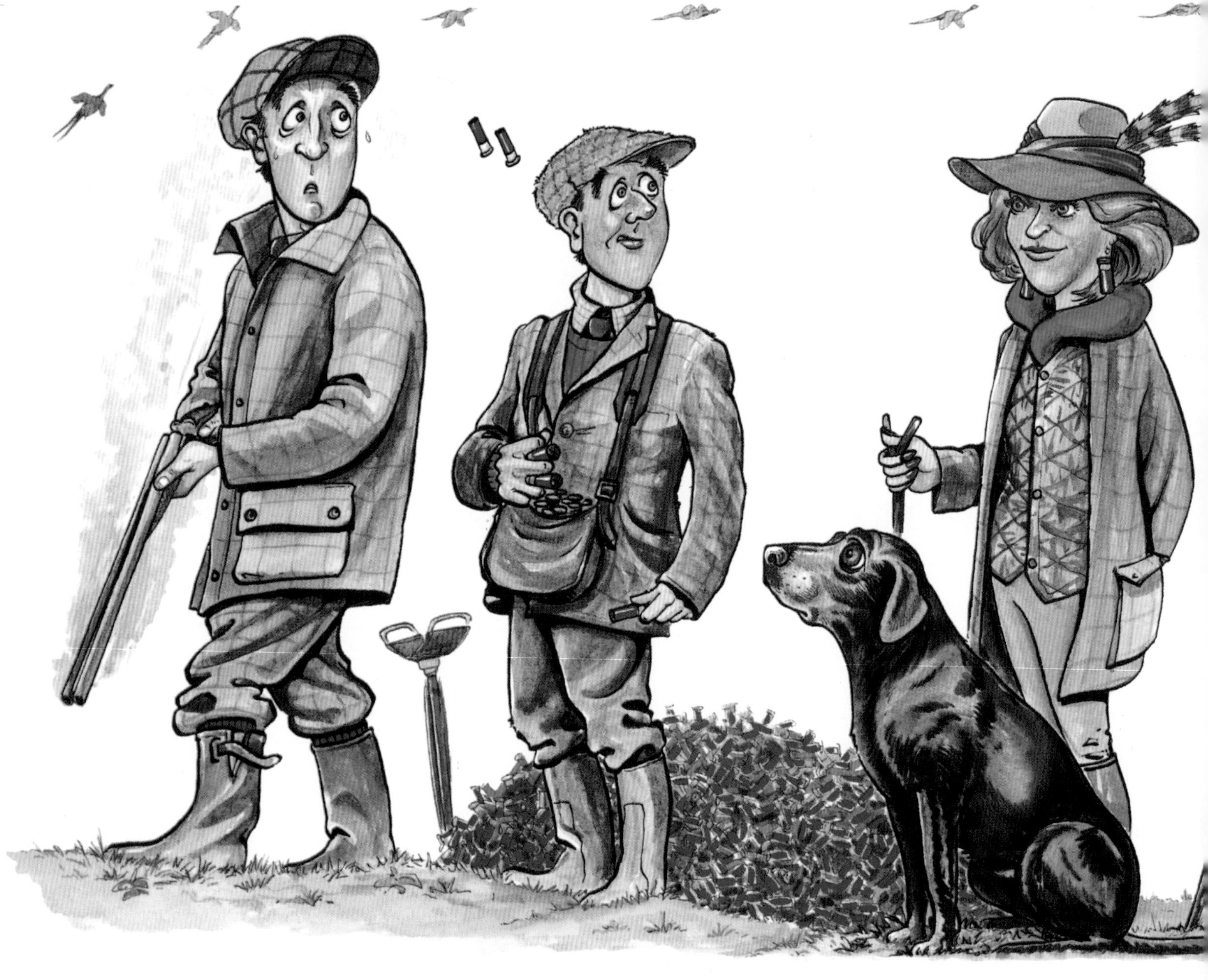

THE OFF DAY

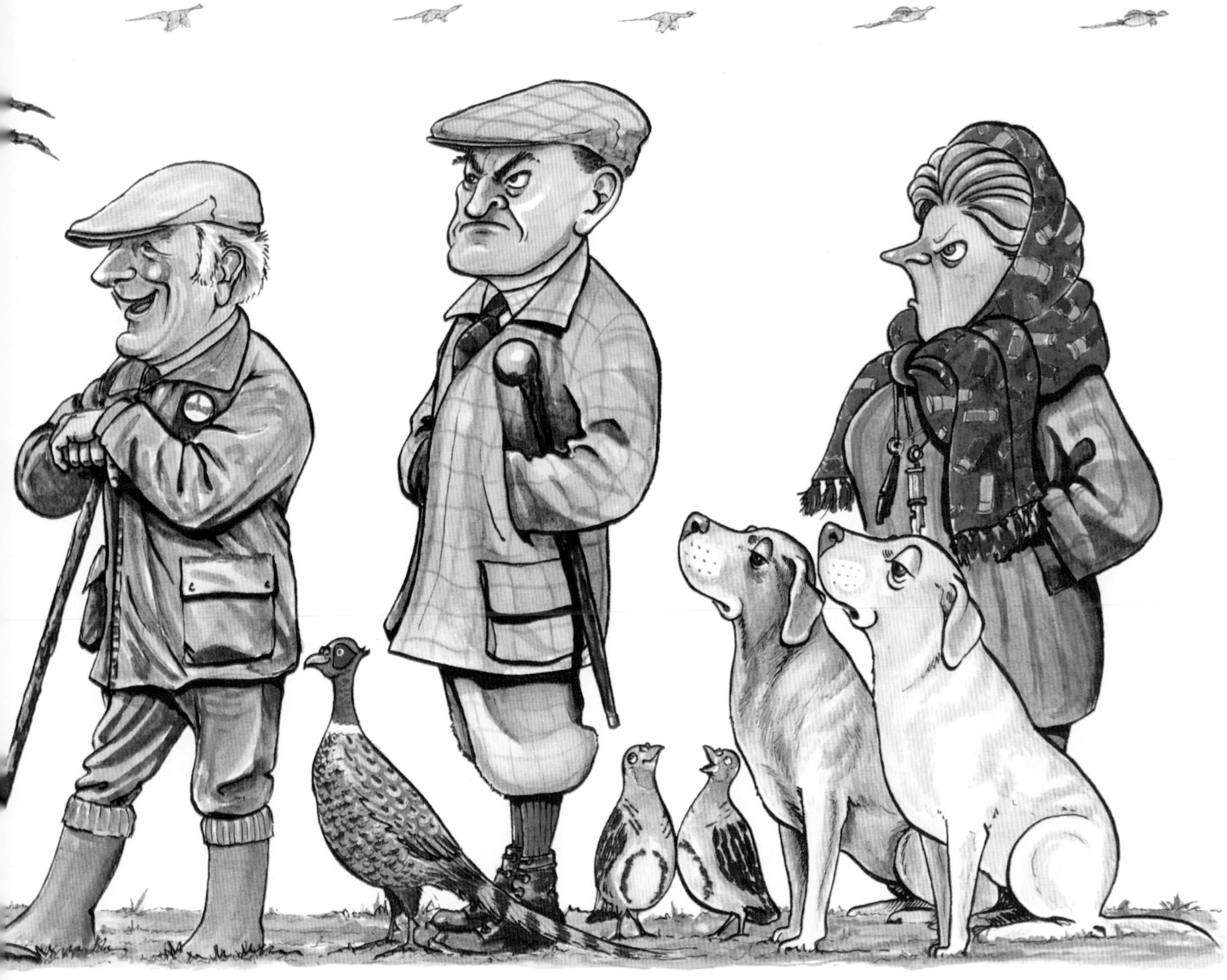

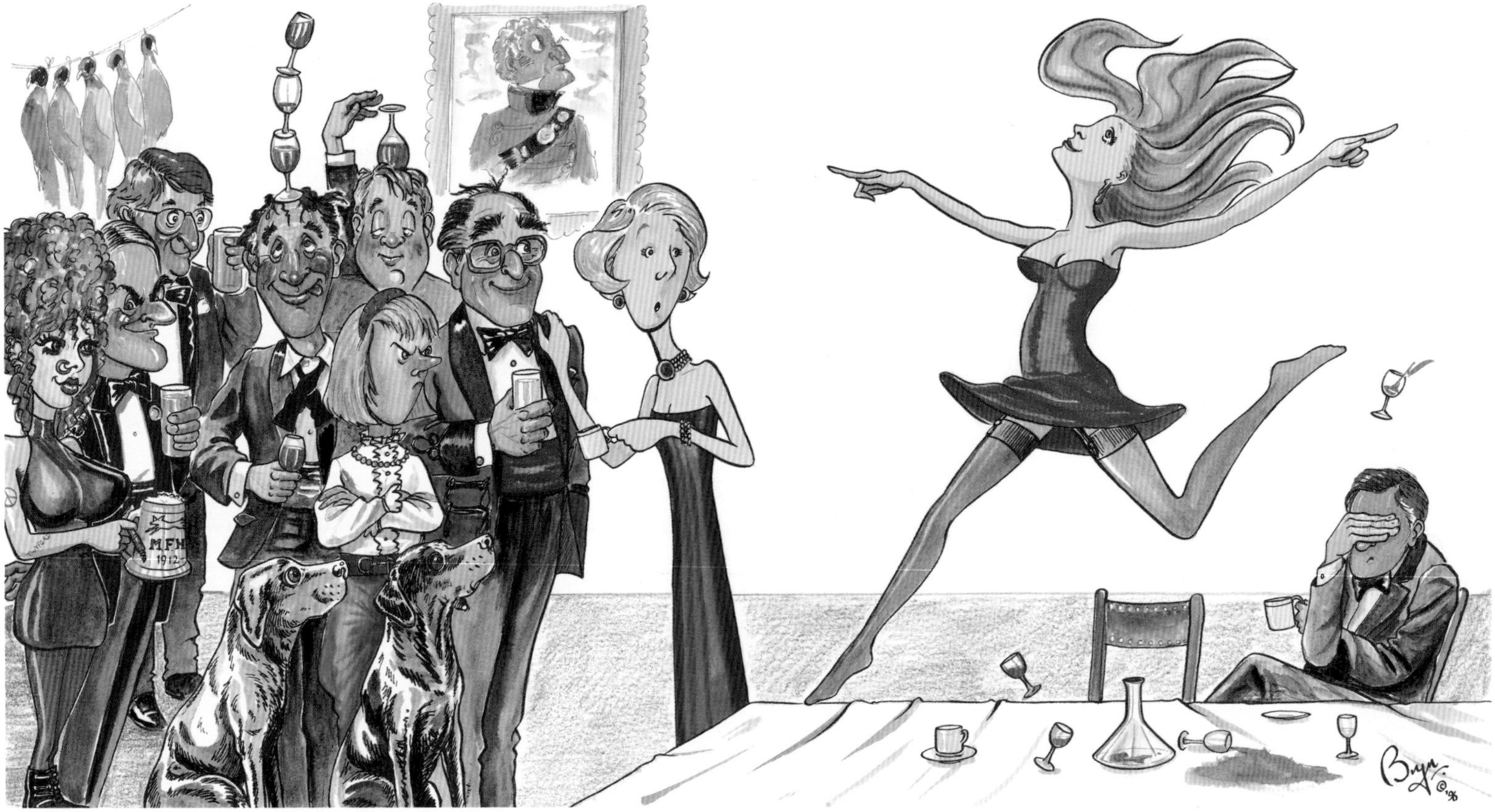
M.F.H.
1912

The Night Before . . . . .

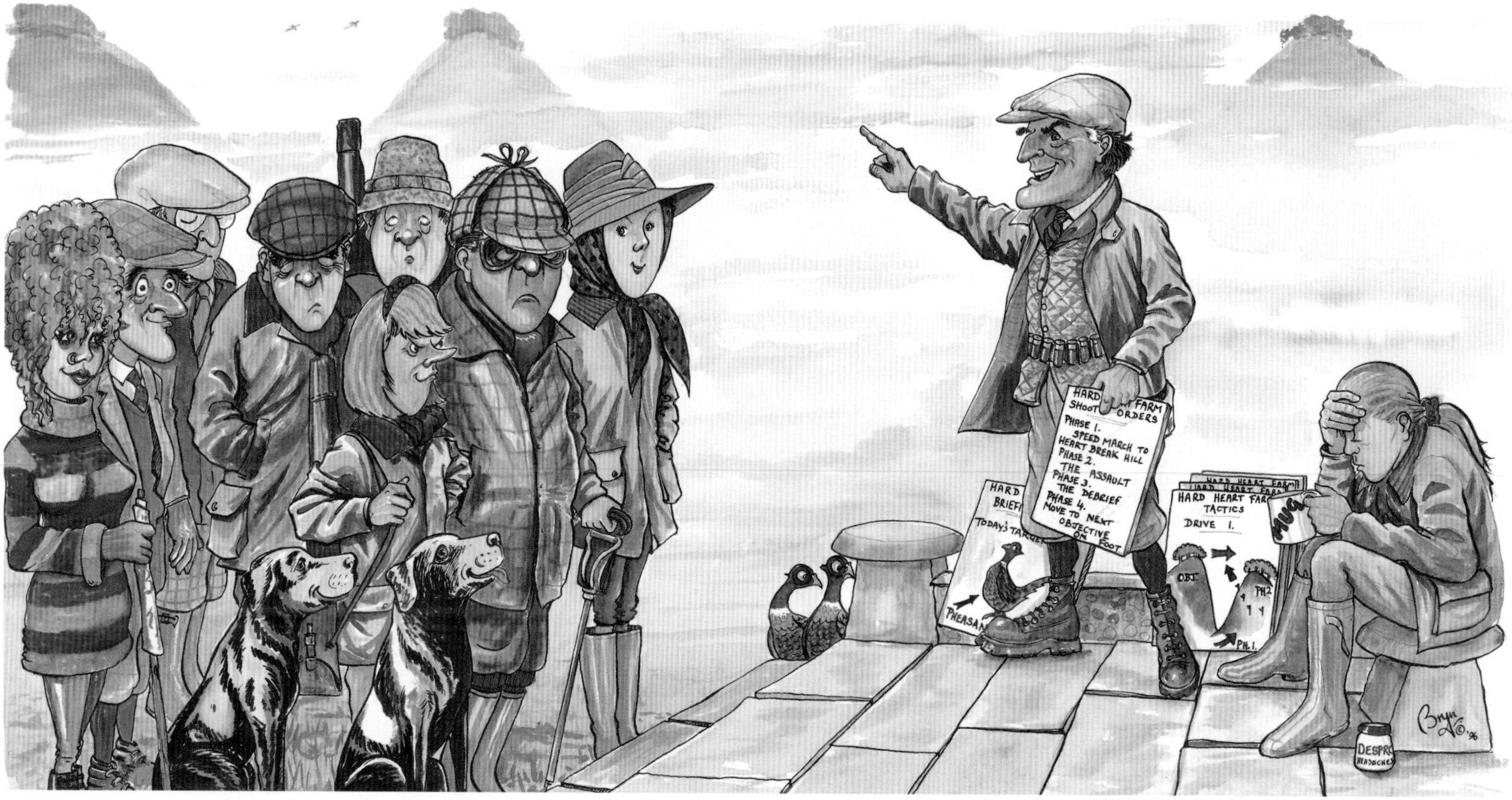
HARD FARM
SHOOT ORDERS
PHASE 1.
SPEED MARCH TO
HEART BREAK HILL
PHASE 2.
THE ASSAULT
PHASE 3.
THE DEBRIEF
PHASE 4.
MOVE TO NEXT
OBJECTIVE
ON FOOT.
HARD
BRIEF
TODAY'S
HARD HEART
TACTICS
DRIVE 1.
OBJ.
PH2
PH.1.
MUG

..... The Morning After

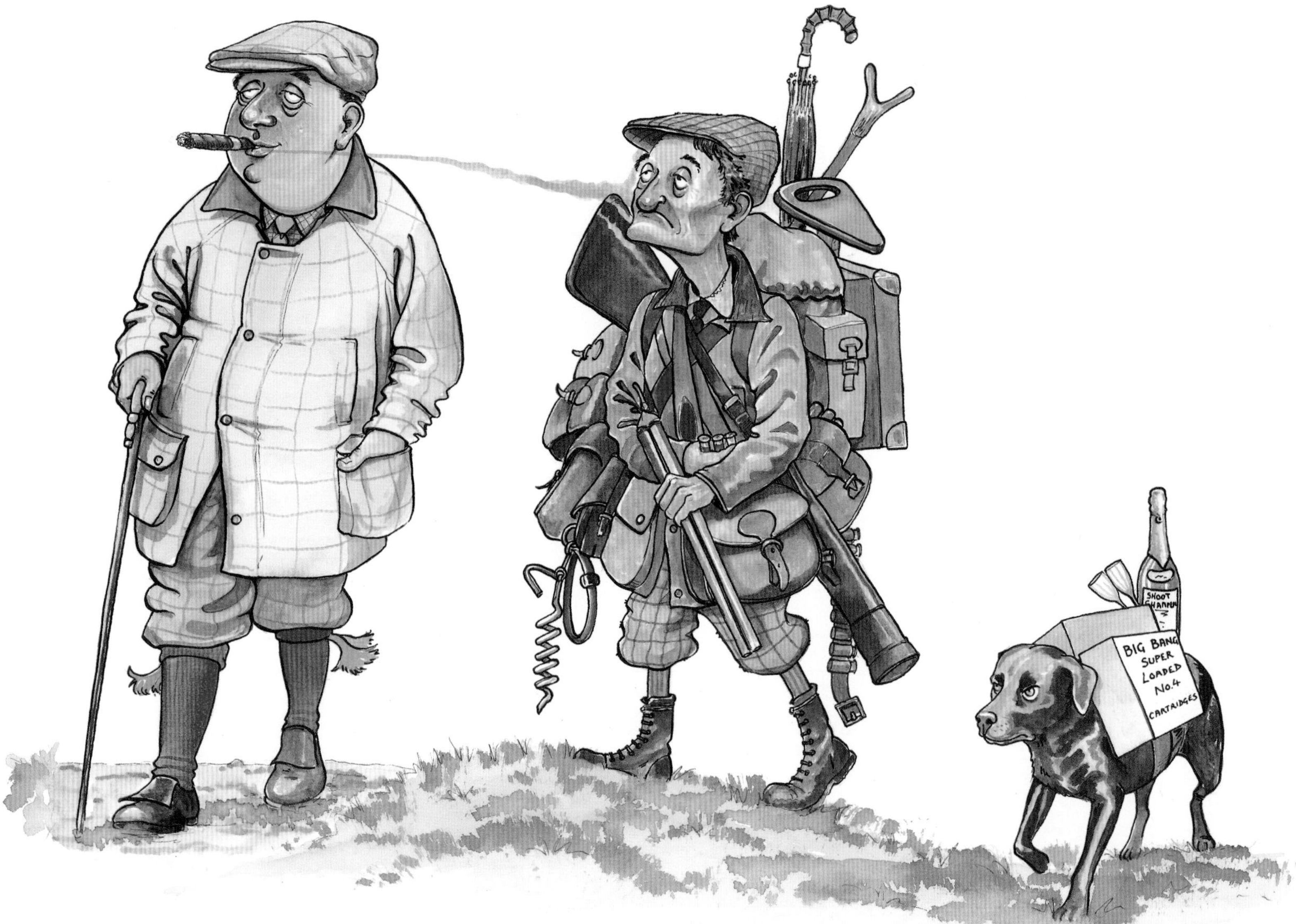
SHOOT
BIG BANG
SUPER
LOADED
No.4
CARTRIDGES

The Support Team

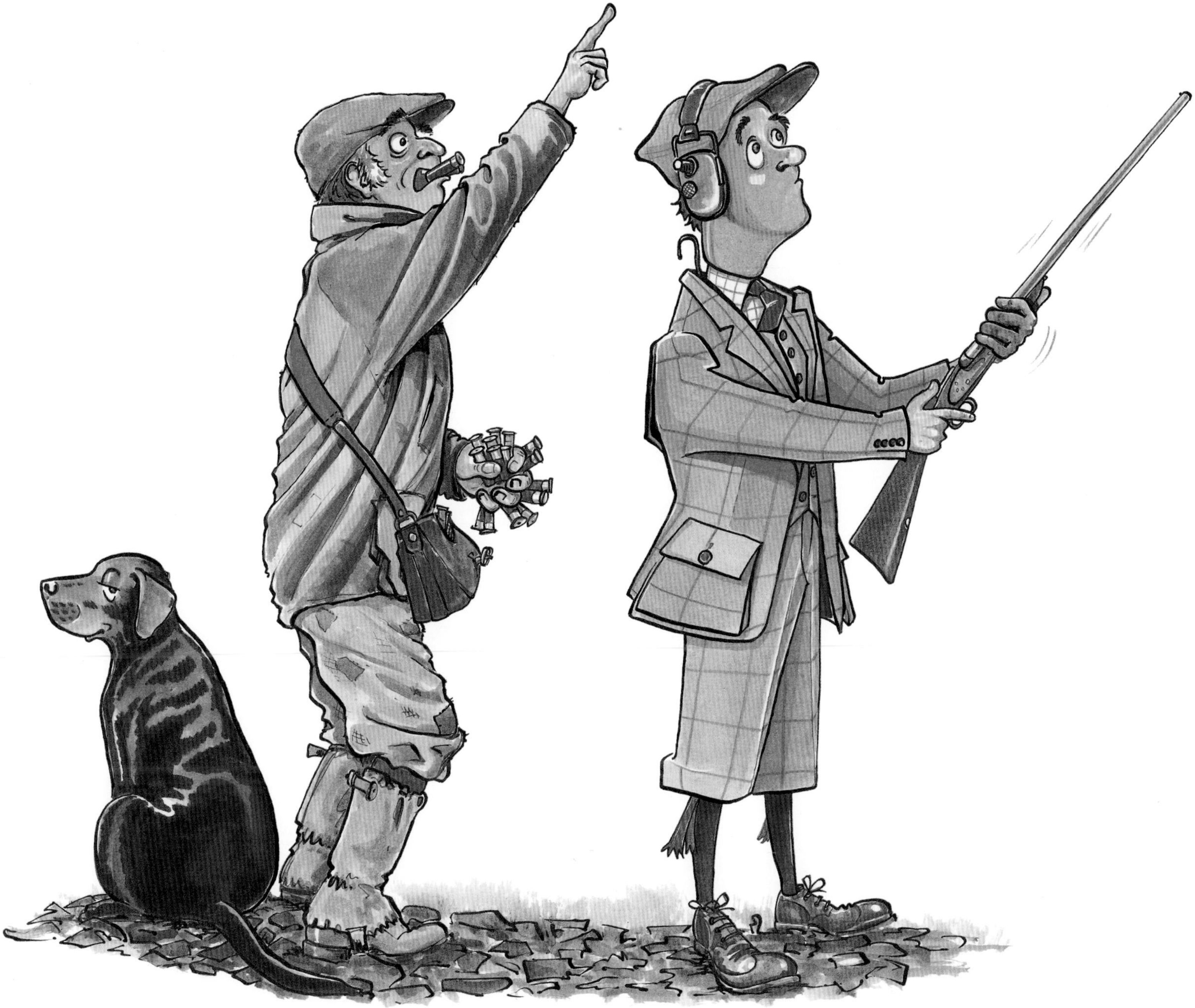

The New Whistle

SECOND BARREL

THE EYE WIPER

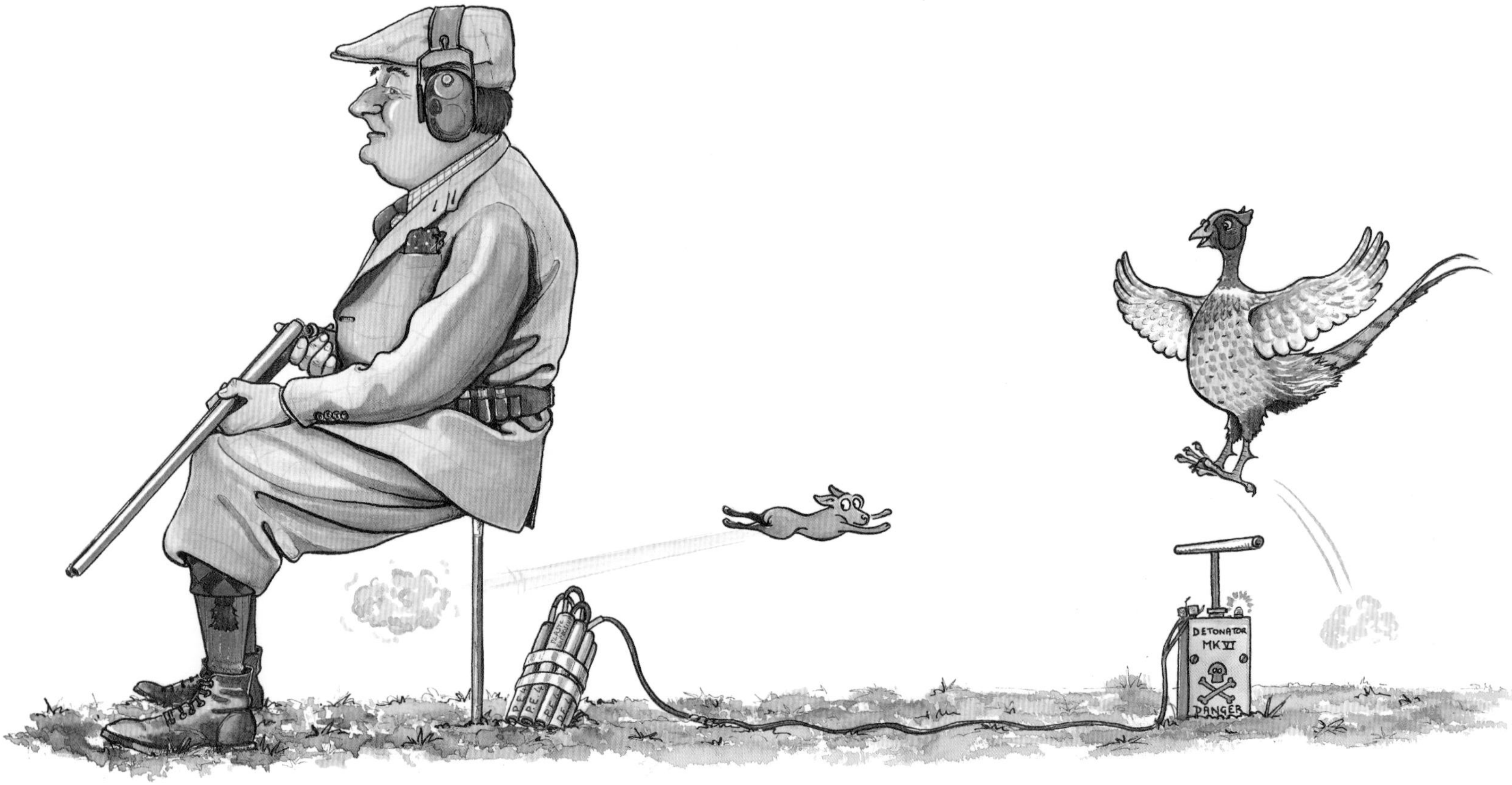
DETONATOR
MK VI
DANGER

Caught Behind

'FOR GOODNESS' SAKE, WILL YOU STOP THAT GHASTLY NOISE!'

TEAMWORK

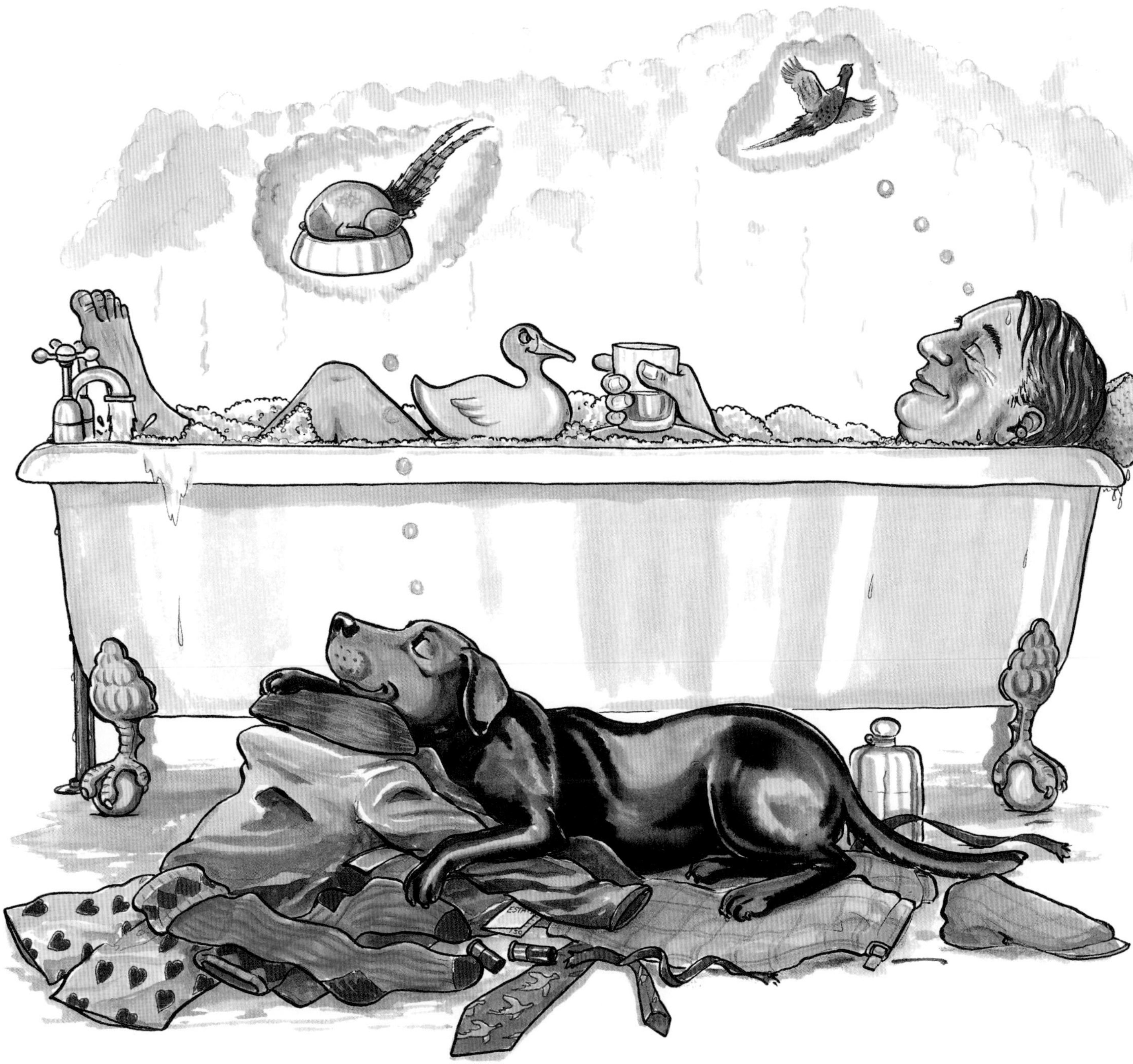

BATH BIRD

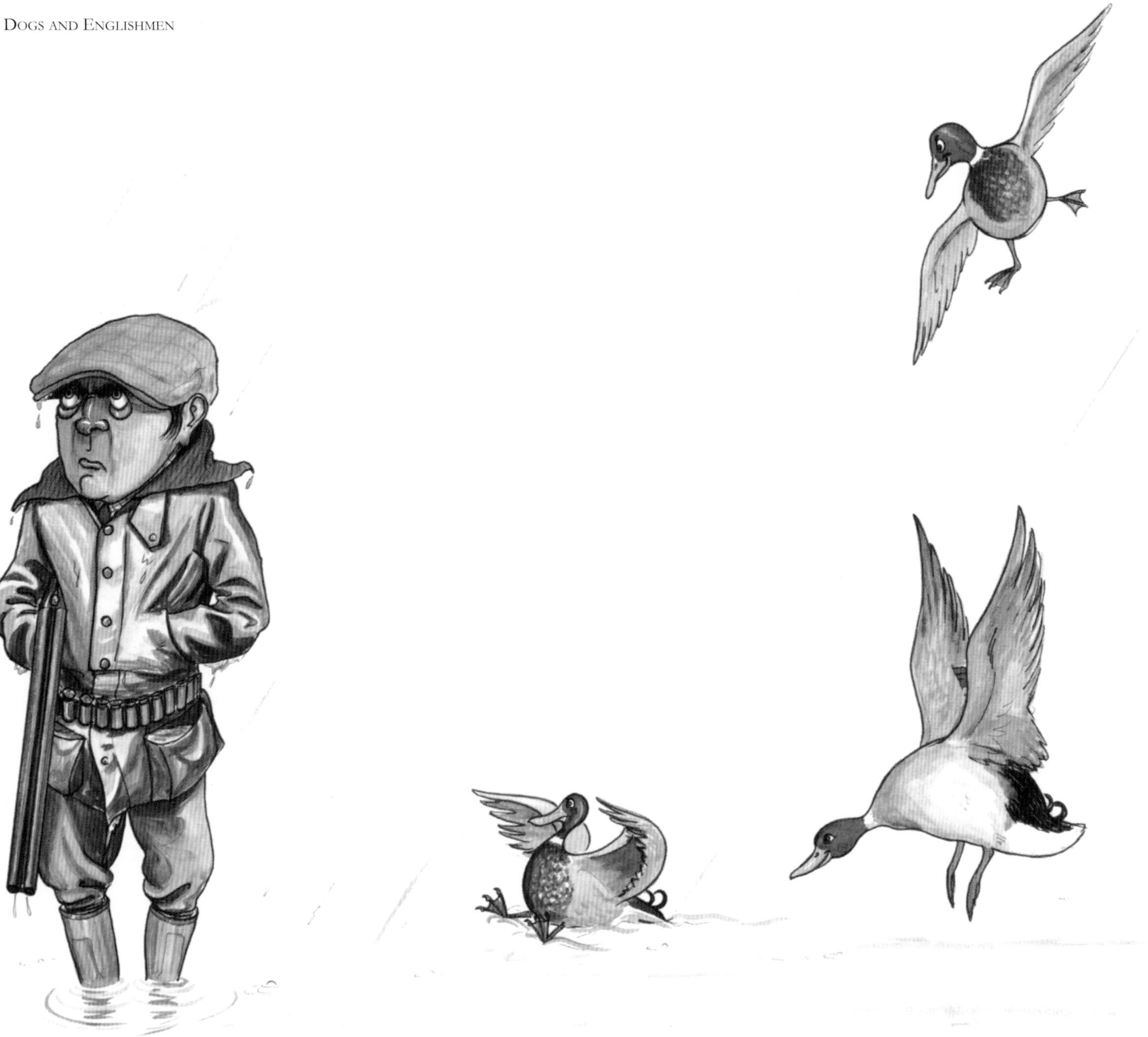

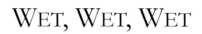

Wet, Wet, Wet

SHOOTING PRACTICE

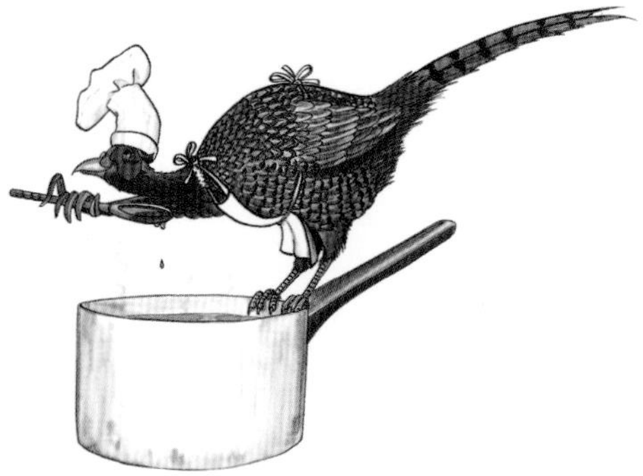

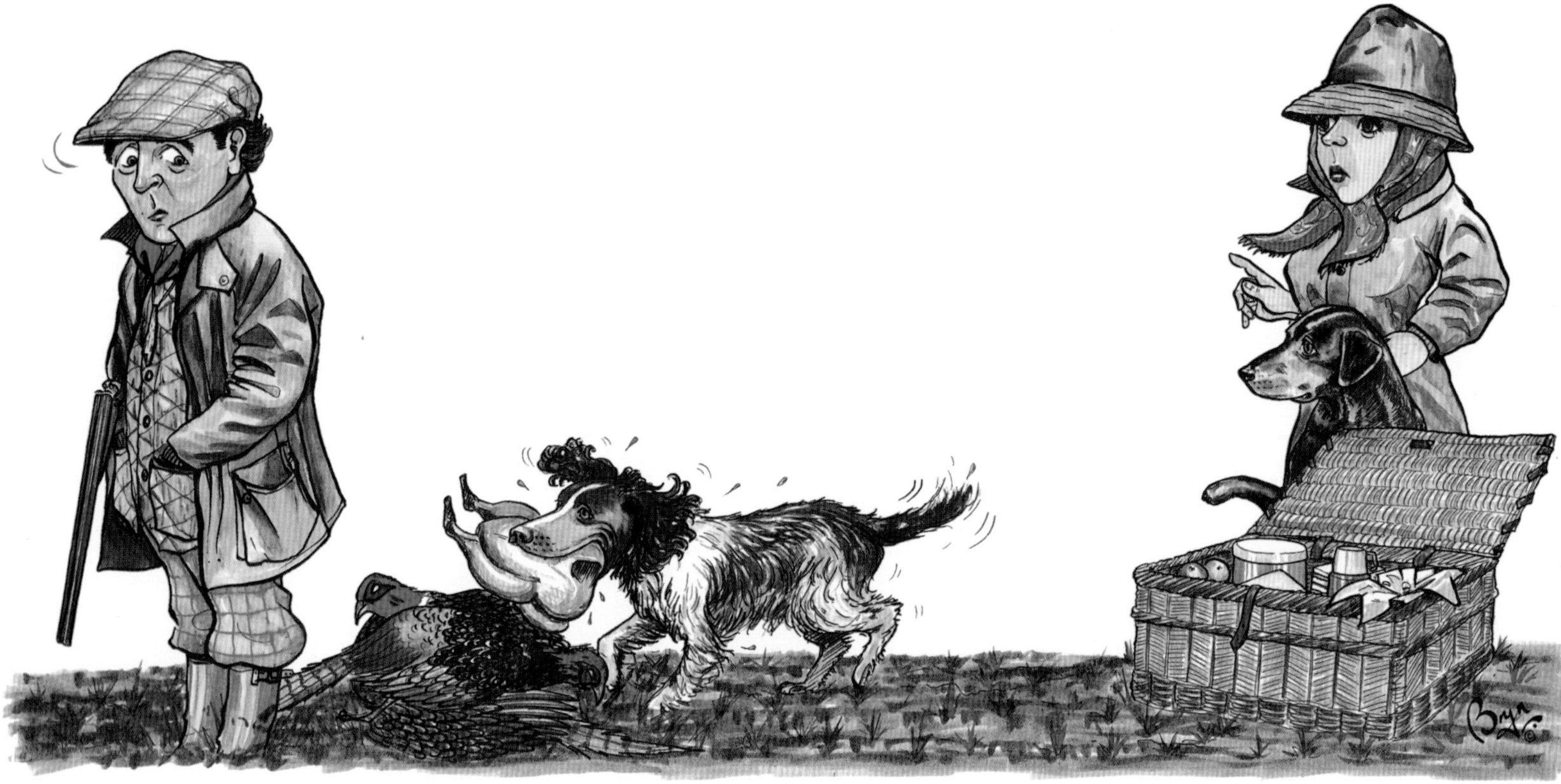

Shoot Lunch

Invitation

Anticipation

Precipitation

Participation

Desperation

Compensation

THE SHOOTING DAY

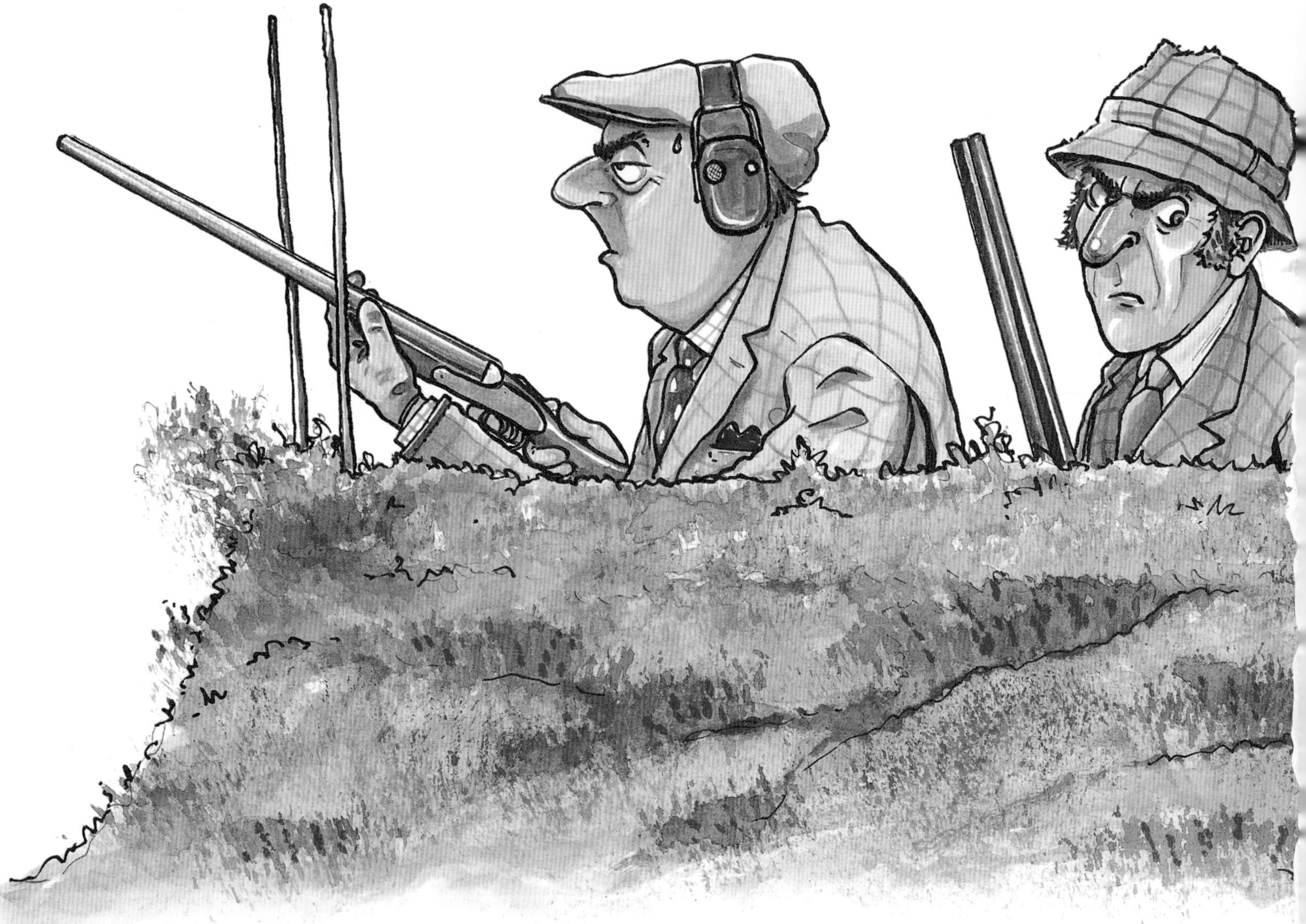

The Glorious Twelfth

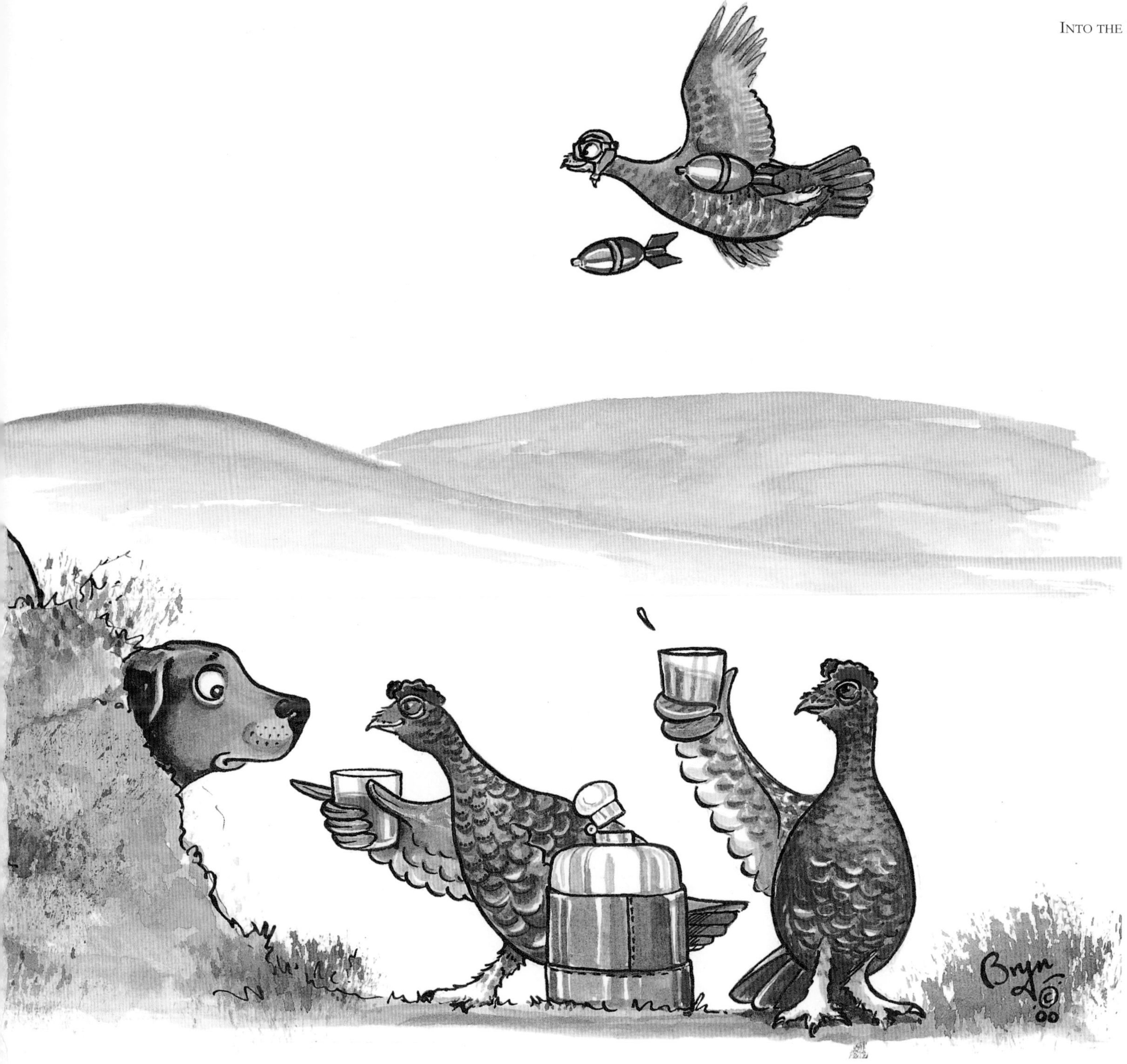
Bryn

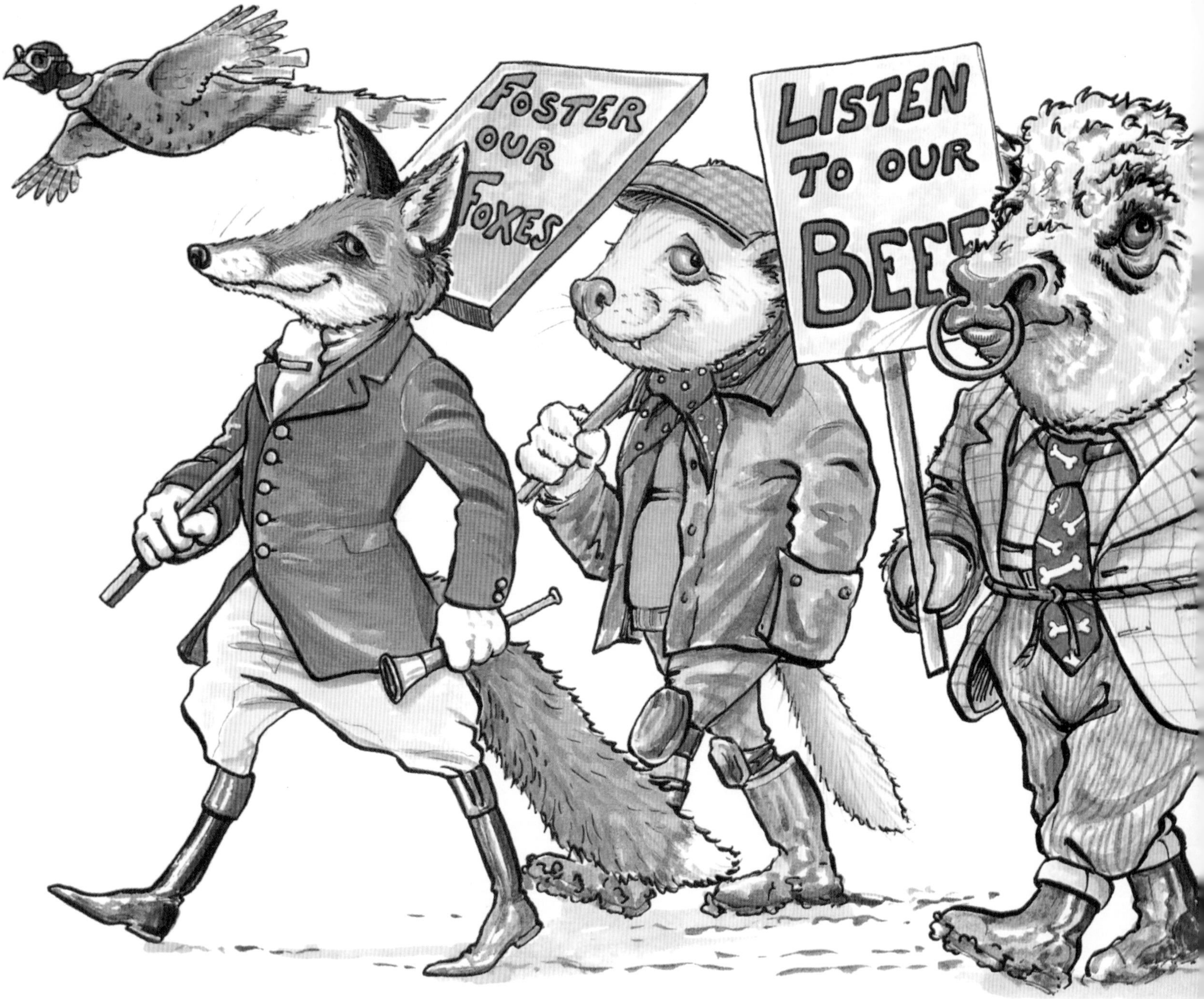
FOSTER OUR FOXES
LISTEN TO OUR BEEF

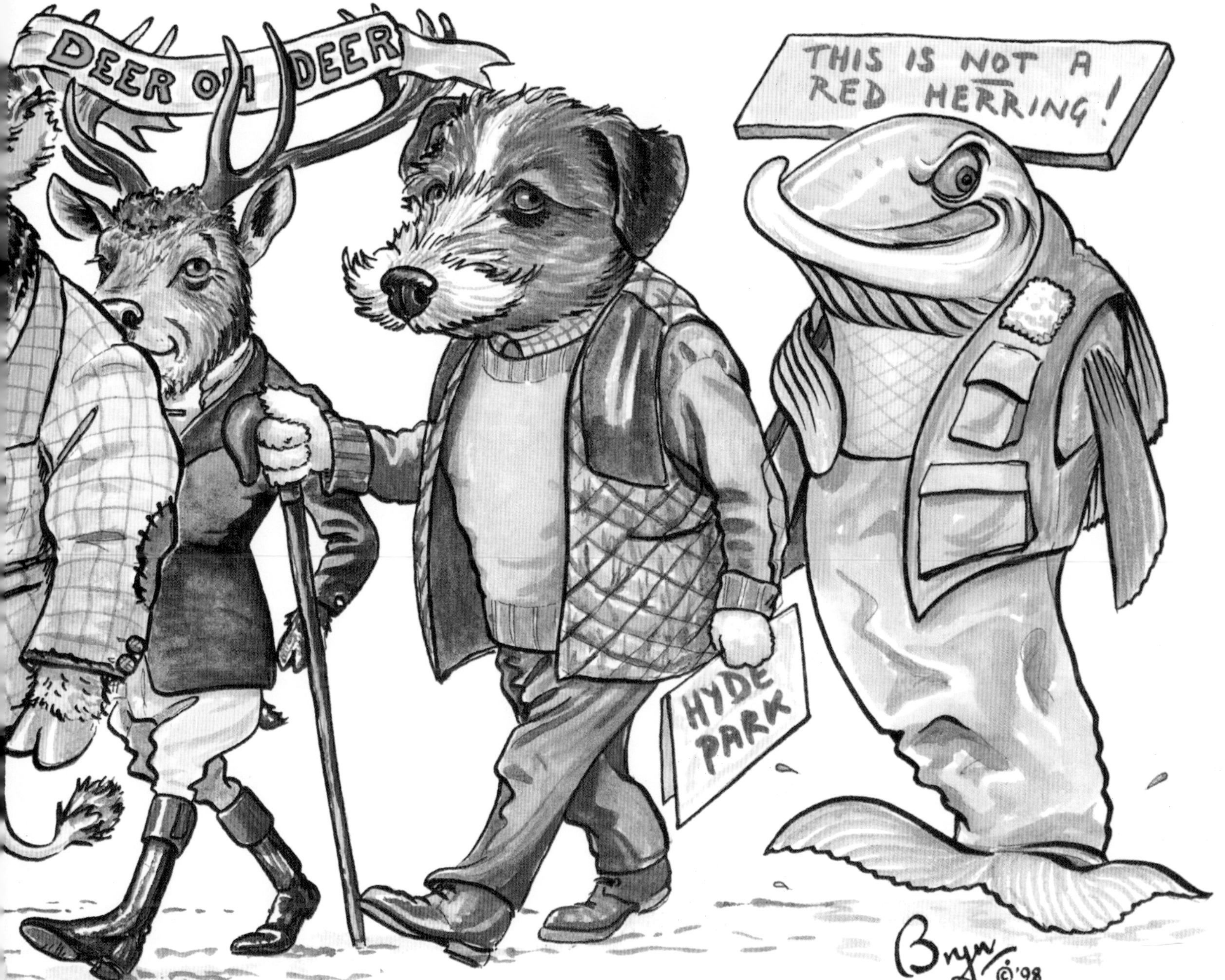
DEER OH DEER
THIS IS NOT A RED HERRING!
HYDE PARK
Bryn ©'98

The Countryside March

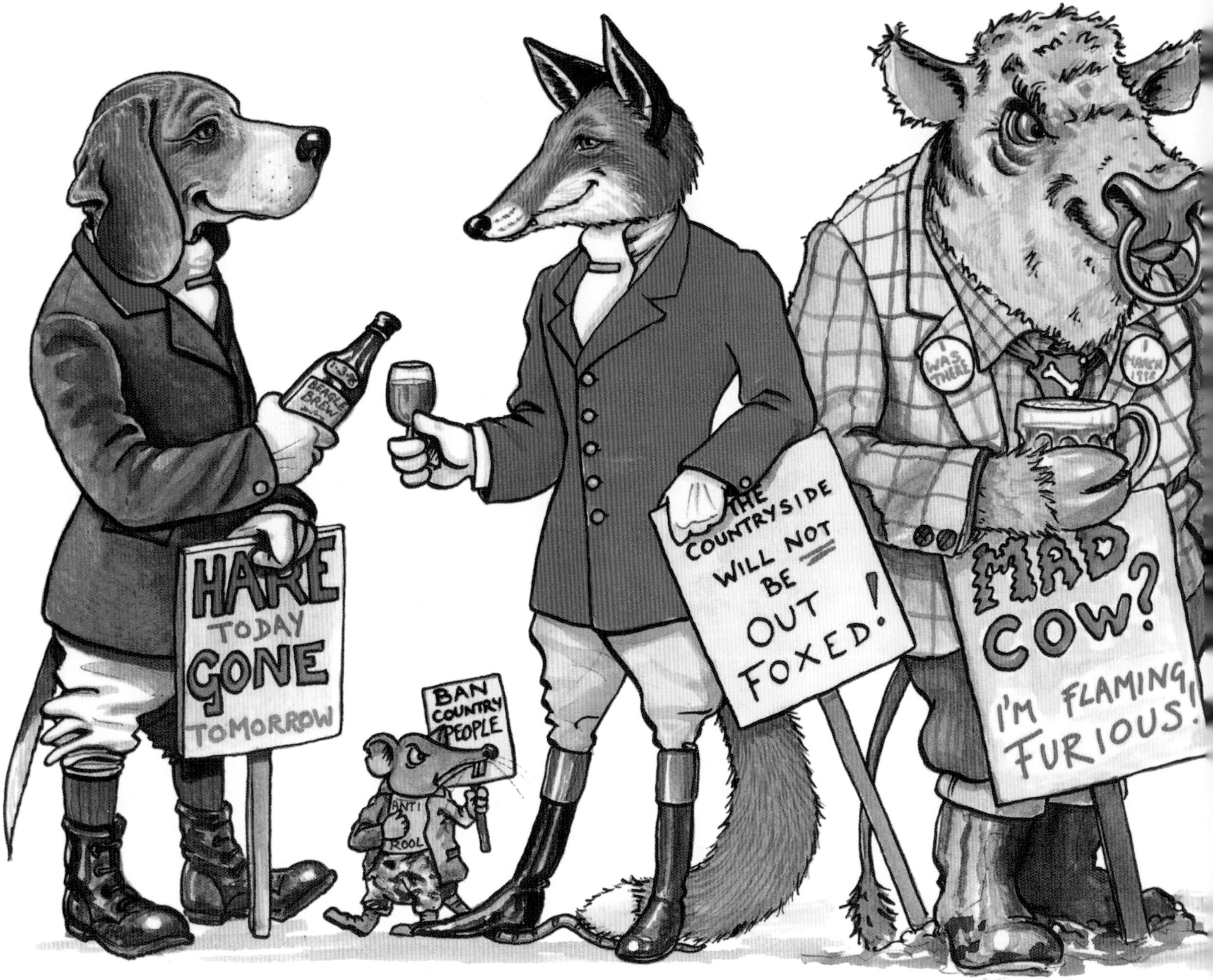
BEAGLE BREW
HARE TODAY GONE TOMORROW
BAN COUNTRY PEOPLE
THE COUNTRYSIDE WILL NOT BE OUT FOXED!
I WAS THERE
MAD COW? I'M FLAMING FURIOUS!

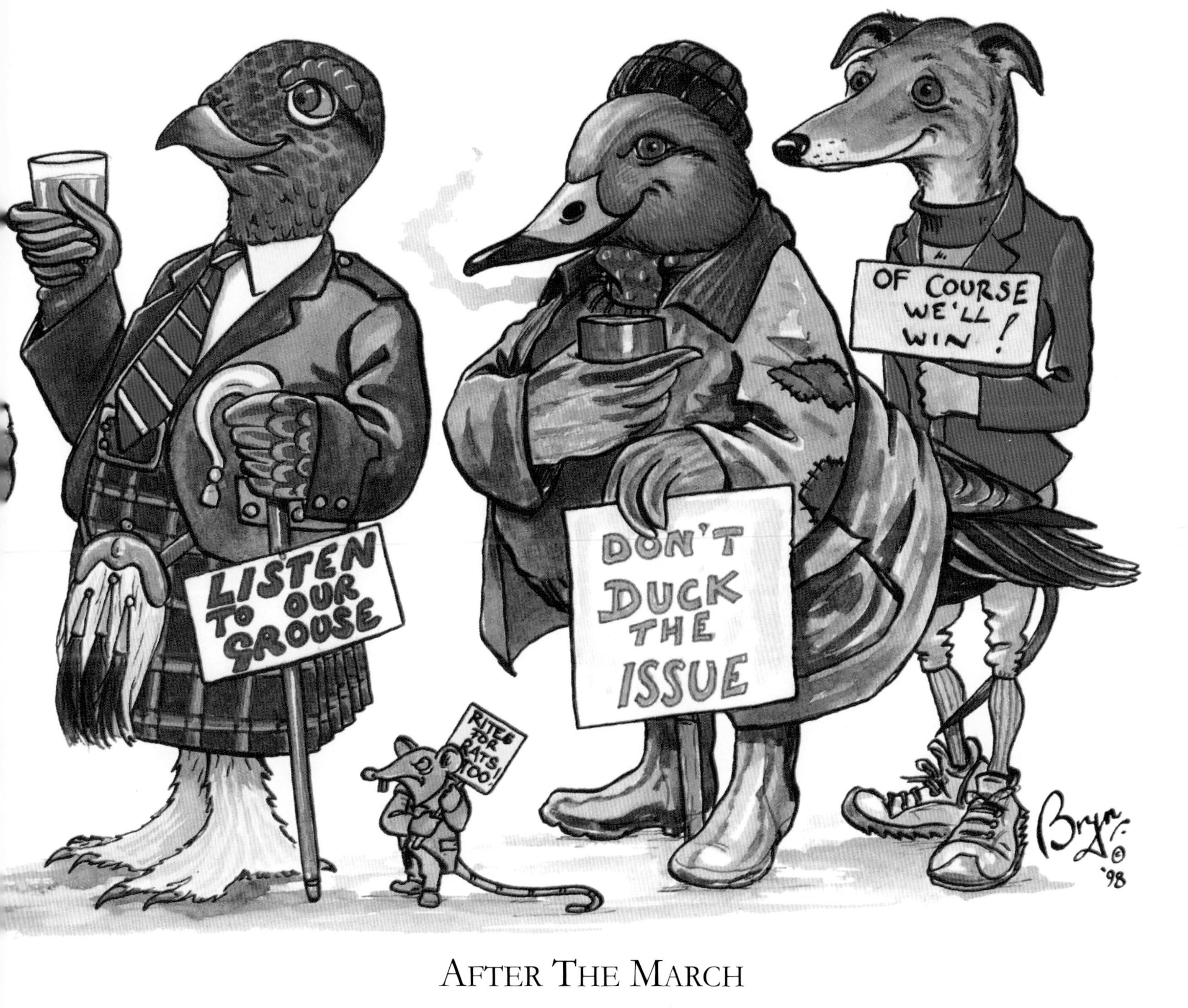
OF COURSE WE'LL WIN!
LISTEN TO OUR GROUSE
DON'T DUCK THE ISSUE
RITES FOR RATS TOO!
Bryn © '98

After The March

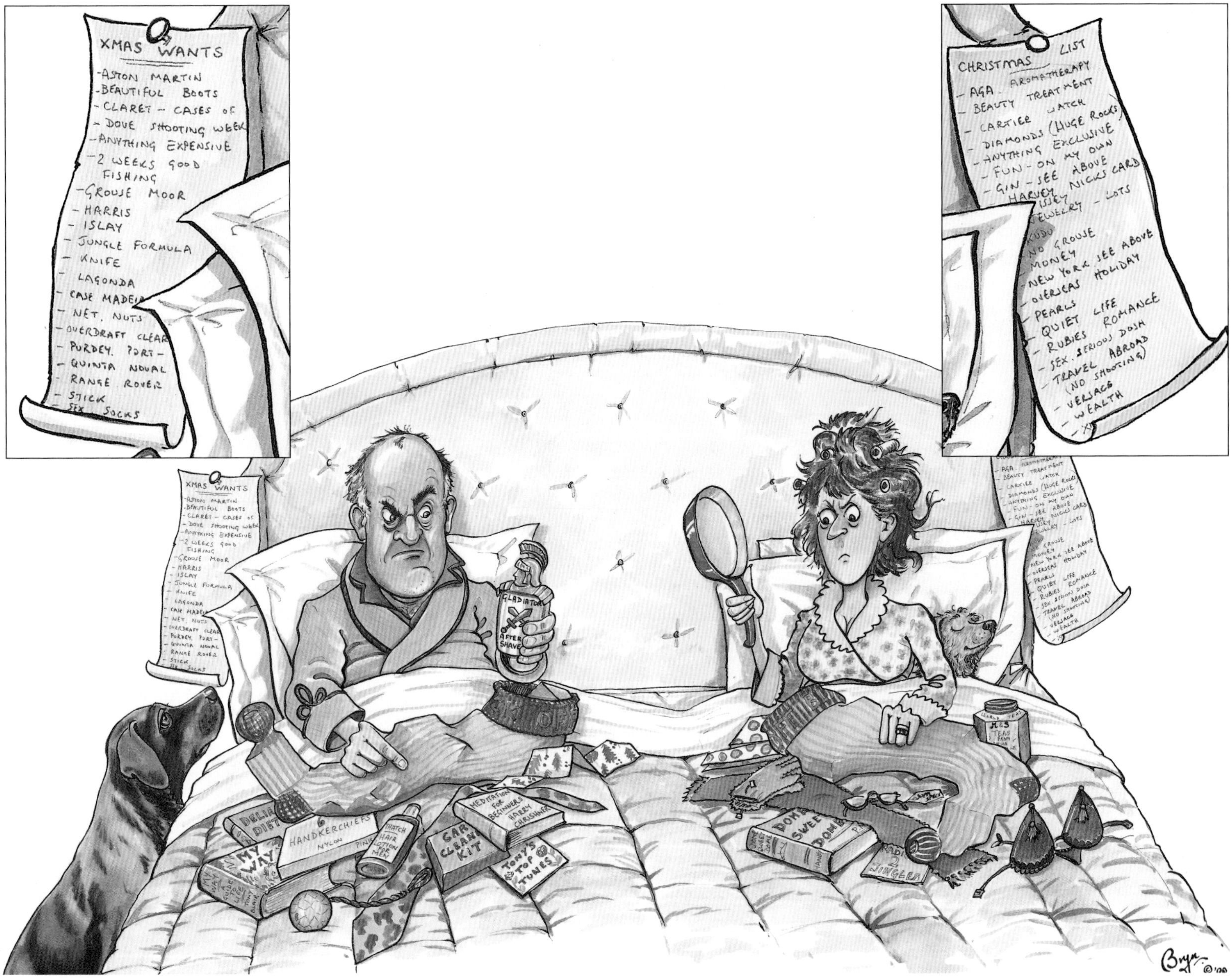
XMAS WANTS
-ASTON MARTIN
-BEAUTIFUL BOOTS
-CLARET – CASES OF
-DOVE SHOOTING WEEK
-ANYTHING EXPENSIVE
-2 WEEKS GOOD FISHING
-GROUSE MOOR
-HARRIS
-ISLAY
-JUNGLE FORMULA
-KNIFE
-LAGONDA
-CASE MADEI
-NET. NUTS
-OVERDRAFT CLEAR
-PURDEY. PORT
-QUINTA NOVAL
-RANGE ROVER
-STICK
-SEX SOCKS
CHRISTMAS LIST
-AGA. AROMATHERAPY
-BEAUTY TREATMENT
-CARTIER WATCH
-DIAMONDS (HUGE ROCKS)
-ANYTHING EXCLUSIVE
-FUN – ON MY OWN
-GIN – SEE ABOVE
HARVEY NICKS CARD
-JEWELRY – LOTS
-NO GROUSE
-MONEY
-NEW YORK SEE ABOVE
-OVERSEAS HOLIDAY
-PEARLS
-QUIET LIFE
-RUBIES ROMANCE
-SEX. SERIOUS DOSH
-TRAVEL ABROAD (NO SHOOTING)
-VERSACE
-WEALTH
GLADIATOR AFTER SHAVE
HANDKERCHIEFS
NYLON
MY WAY
CAR CLEAN KIT
TONY'S TOP TUNES
MEDITATION FOR BEGINNERS
DOMB SWEET DOMB
JINGLES

THE CHRISTMAS LIST

EVERYONE WAS LOOKING FORWARD TO GIGGLY SUPS WITH MRS AGA

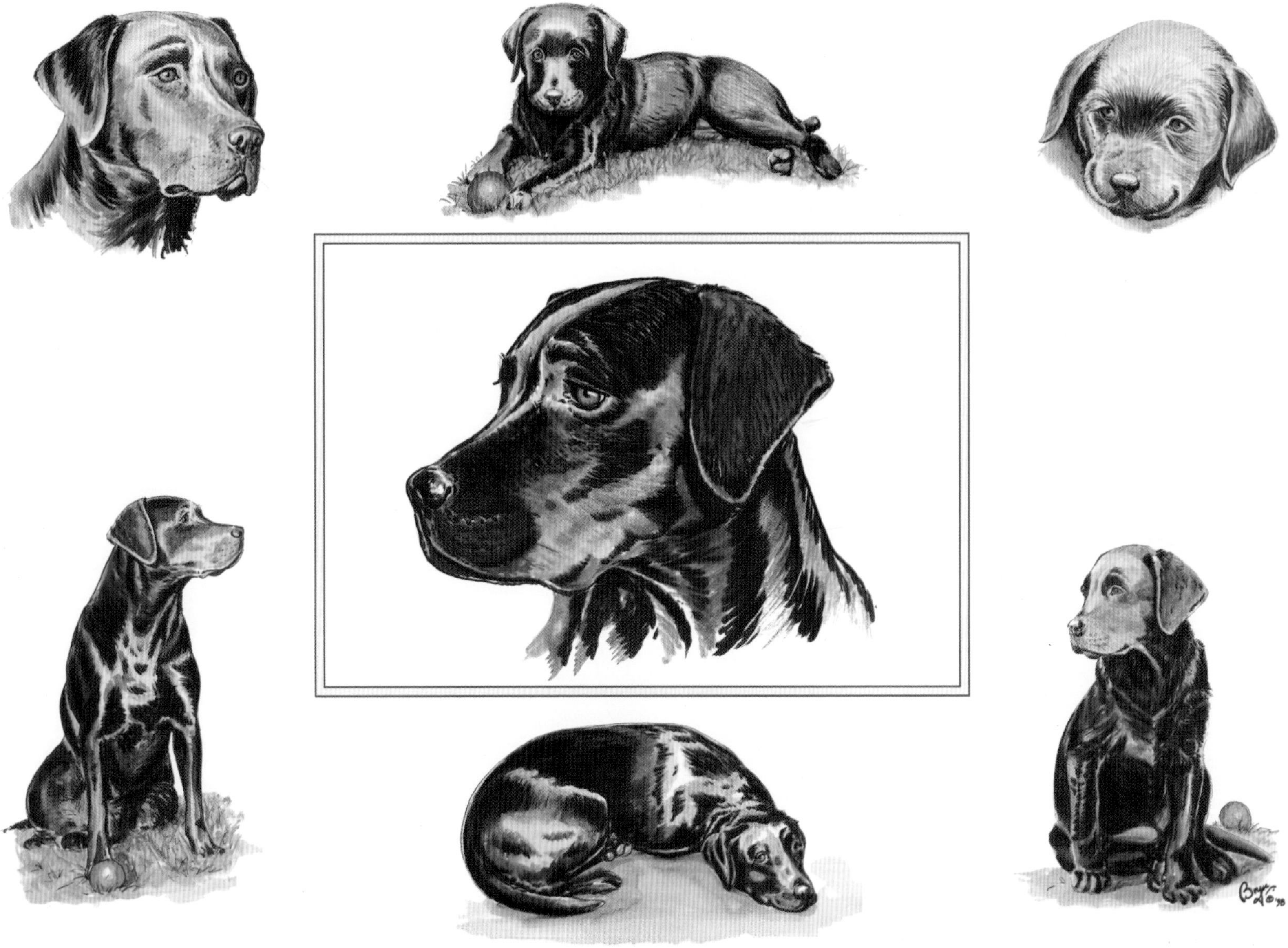

Mango the Magnificent